WITHDRAWN

WINNIPEG

JAN

D0707829

100 NATURE HOT SPOTS IN ONTARIO

100 NATURE HOT SPOTS IN ONTARIO

The Best Parks, Conservation Areas and Wild Places

Chris Earley and Tracy C. Read
With Kyle Horner, Owen Bjorgan and Justin Peter

FIREFLY BOOKS

A FIREFLY BOOK

Published by Firefly Books Ltd. 2016

Copyright © 2016 Firefly Books Ltd.
Text copyright © 2016 Chris Earley and Tracy C. Read

All rights reserved. No part of this publication may be reproduced, stored in a retrieval system, or transmitted in any form or by any means, electronic, mechanical, photocopying, recording or otherwise, without the prior written permission of the Publisher.

First printing

Publisher Cataloging-in-Publication Data (U.S.)
Names: Earley, Chris G., 1968-, author | Read, Tracy C., author.
Title: 100 nature hot spots in Ontario / Chris Earley and Tracy C. Read.
Description: Richmond Hill, Ontario, Canada : Firefly Books, 2016. | Includes index. |
Summary: "A guidebook to the best nature sites in Ontario categorized by region. It includes special features, location details, color photographs and maps, with suggestions on how to make the most of each site" — Provided by publisher.
Identifiers: ISBN 978-1-77085-705-6 (pbk.)
Subjects: LCSH: Natural history – Ontario — Guidebooks. | Ontario – Description and travel.
Classification: LCC QH106.2.O6E275 |DDC 508.713 – dc23

Library and Archives Canada Cataloguing in Publication
Earley, Chris G., 1968-, author
100 nature hot spots in Ontario : the best parks, conservation areas and wild places / Chris Earley and Tracy C. Read.
Includes index.
ISBN 978-1-77085-705-6 (paperback)
1. Natural areas—Ontario—Guidebooks. 2. Parks—Ontario—Guidebooks. 3. Protected areas—Ontario—Guidebooks. 4. Ontario—Description and travel. I. Read, Tracy C., author II. Title. III. Title: One hundred nature hot spots in Ontario.
FC3057.E27 2016   917.13   C2015-908178-5

Published in the United States by
Firefly Books (U.S.) Inc.
P.O. Box 1338, Ellicott Station
Buffalo, New York 14205

Published in Canada by
Firefly Books Ltd.
50 Staples Avenue, Unit 1
Richmond Hill, Ontario L4B 0A7

Cover and interior design: Hartley Millson

Printed in Canada

The publisher gratefully acknowledges the financial support for our publishing program by the Government of Canada through the Canada Book Fund as administered by the Department of Canadian Heritage.

Dedication

To Alan Watson, for inspiring so many of Ontario's naturalists, including me.
—C.E.

To Adrian Forsyth and Wayne Lynch, two nature lovers who taught me that science is also an art.
—T.C.R.

Acknowledgements

In order to research, write and source photographs for *100 Nature Hot Spots in Ontario: The Best Parks, Conservation Areas and Wild Places*, we depended on the generosity and goodwill of a host of friends, colleagues and strangers. We'd like to thank Richard Aaron, Deanna Abbott-McNeil, Val Aloian, Joe Bartok, Raechel Bonomo, Bob Bowles, Mike Burrell, Tim Cumming, Susan Dickinson, Bruce Di Labio, Frank B. Edwards, Frances Farmer, Judy Hammond, Shelley Hunt, Pete Kelly, Janice McLean, Troy McMullin, Glenn Perrett, Sarah Rupert and Alan Watson. Our thanks as well to Firefly's Lionel Koffler and Michael Worek for enthusiastically supporting the project, and to designer Hartley Millson, for his keen eye, patience and positive energy.

We also relied on the staffs at a number of groups and agencies for their assistance and expertise. These included the Ausable Bayfield Conservation Authority; Credit Valley Conservation; Essex Region Conservation Authority; Friends of Seaton Trail; Hamilton Conservation Authority; Nottawasaga Valley Conservation Authority; Ojibway Nature Centre; Ontario Nature; Ontario Parks; Queen's University Biological Station; Royal Botanical Gardens; Saugeen Valley Conservation Authority; and the Wye Marsh Wildlife Centre and their partners, Burlington's Trumpeter Swan Coalition. We want to offer a warm thanks to the Nature Conservancy of Canada, which does invaluable work to protect and preserve the country's areas of natural diversity. Many NCC projects appear in *100 Nature Hot Spots in Ontario*. To learn more about the NCC, please visit their website at natureconservancycanada.ca.

Finally, we'd like to express our appreciation for co-contributors Kyle Horner, Owen Bjorgan and Justin Peters, who so skillfully shared their insights and passion for the natural world in *100 Nature Hot Spots in Ontario*.

—Chris Earley and Tracy C. Read

Contents

10   Southwestern Ontario

72   Central Ontario South

102   Niagara Region

Introduction

The name "Ontario" was derived from an Iroquois word that roughly translates as "beautiful water," and indeed, there's no shortage of water here. The province boasts hundreds of thousands of waterways, including the Great Lakes—the largest group of freshwater lakes in the world—as well as the countless rivers, lakes, ponds and wetlands that characterize the Canadian Shield, which occupies more than half of the province's landmass. In addition to water, there are 70 million hectares of forests, from the remnant deciduous Carolinian forest in southern Ontario and the Great Lakes-St. Lawrence forest in central Ontario to northern Ontario's boreal forest and Hudson Bay's lowland forest.

Other landforms help define the landscape as well. The massive Niagara Escarpment charges its way across central Ontario, up the Bruce Peninsula and over Georgian Bay's Manitoulin Island. In eastern Ontario, the Laurentian Highlands stretch into Algonquin Provincial Park as the Opeongo Hills; the Canadian Shield, on its way south to merge with the Adirondacks, pops up again as the Thousand Islands. Along the shores of the Great Lakes are windswept sandy beaches—rocks, crystals and seashells that have eroded over time through the action of wind, water and ice. Wherever you look in Ontario, you'll see the legacy of North America's ancient beginnings.

It all adds up to a breathtakingly rich collection of ecosystems and land types that supports some 3,600 species of plants, 483 species of birds, 80 species of mammals, 150 species of fish and 50 species of amphibians and reptiles. It also creates an abundance of family-friendly destinations with appeal for birdwatchers, botanists, biologists, budding naturalists, photographers, hikers, campers and paddlers. We hope you'll find *100 Nature Hot Spots in Ontario: The Best Parks, Conservation Areas and Wild Places* an engaging introduction to Ontario's natural wonders, many of which are right in your backyard.

In gathering hot-spot recommendations from colleagues and friends, we learned about out-of-the-way natural gems and discovered fresh information about places we thought we knew. But as we honed our list, we realized we were destined to leave out a host of favourite places—the sheer natural bounty of Ontario makes that inevitable. If you don't find a favourite park, nature reserve or wild place here, perhaps knowing that we haven't increased the traffic to your preferred refuge will be a small consolation.

That so much of Ontario's wilderness is protected is thanks, in large part, to our provincial and national park systems, which affirm the importance of preserving wild space for all of us. Regional authorities develop and protect conservation areas and nature reserves, but the grassroots work of naturalists who rehabilitate and protect discrete ecosystems is also a critical piece of this story. Volunteer stewards of the land spend their time making inventories of plants and animals, forging and maintaining trails and doing educational outreach. The message they share is that the Earth's future depends on how well we defend our healthy waterways, mature forests and habitat and species diversity. Generous landowners who donate their property to not-for-profit groups like the Nature Conservancy of Canada also play an essential role.

In this guide, we've tried to highlight the strengths of each of our 100 spots and to sketch its appeal for a range of visitors. The book is organized by region, and the entries within each region are presented alphabetically. Depending on where you live, some destinations will be close at hand, while others may require a weekend trip or more. A visit to some may involve a vigorous hike or cycle, others only a contemplative stroll along a boardwalk or trail. Still others are better investigated from the water, where a kayak or canoe provides access to shorelines and the animals and plants that make their living there. But one thing is certain: Each one has something uncommon to offer the nature-loving visitor.

Wherever you visit, keep in mind that exploring nature always involves respecting your surroundings. Unless otherwise indicated, stay on the prescribed paths (fragile flora often grows alongside the trails and can easily be damaged). Go to the destination's website before your visit to check for holiday closings and to make sure that no other activities are scheduled (some places allow seasonal hunting). Always remember that you're a guest in a place inhabited by other creatures—do your best not to disturb their world.

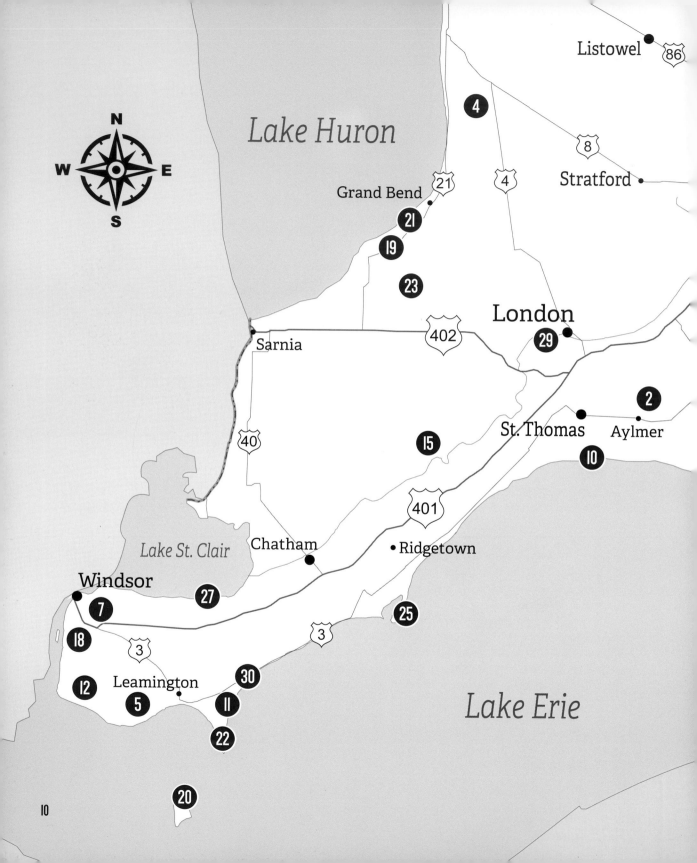

Listowel

Lake Huron

Grand Bend

Stratford

London

Sarnia

St. Thomas

Aylmer

Lake St. Clair

Chatham

Ridgetown

Windsor

Leamington

Lake Erie

10

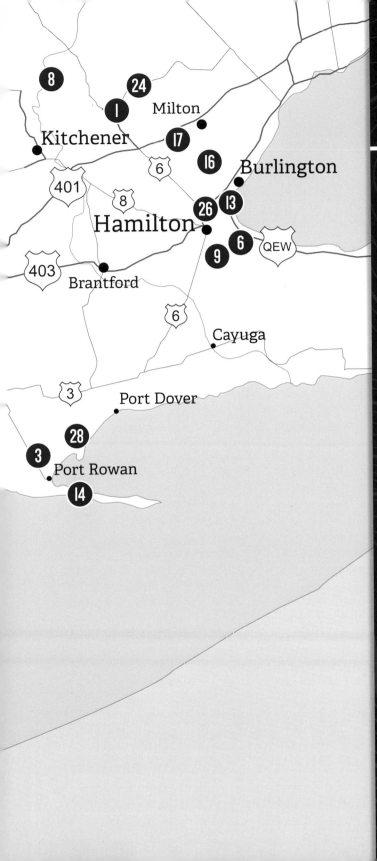

Southwestern Ontario

The Arboretum, University of Guelph

Explore old-growth forest and learn how to identify native trees and attract wildlife to your own backyard

What Makes This Hot Spot Hot?

- Visitors can find almost every native Ontario tree species in one place.
- Each September, courtesy of the Auxiliary Plant Sale, visitors can buy and take home their own rare tree.
- At the Gosling Wildlife Gardens, visitors learn how to make their own backyard a wildlife haven.

Address: The Arboretum, University of Guelph, Guelph, ON N1G 2W1
Tel.: (519) 824-4120 ext. 52113
Website: uoguelph. ca/arboretum

Open year-round

The culmination of an idea first proposed in 1939, The Arboretum at the University of Guelph at last started to take shape in 1970, when supporters of the "living laboratory" began to establish and nurture a diversity of trees and shrubs. Today, The Arboretum has one of the best collections of northern hemisphere woody plants in Canada. But its real claim to fame is its collection of Ontario rare woody plants, among them the cucumber tree (the only magnolia species native to Canada), cherry birch, pawpaw, eastern flowering dogwood and Shumard oak. These species and many others are all part of The Arboretum's Rare Woody Plant Gene Bank, a living gene bank that enables restoration projects across Ontario to plant saplings grown from local seed sources. The site's

Native Trees of Ontario trail alone features almost every native tree found in the province, accompanied by descriptive signs that teach visitors how to identify each species.

Besides these remarkable plant collections, The Arboretum's 165 hectares comprise three old-growth forests, many old fields and a class-one provincially significant wetland, all within Guelph's city limits. With over 100 lichen species, more than 200 bird species, over 275 species of fungus and almost 800 moth species, it is an incredibly biodiverse area. The sheer variety of habitats in combination with some 10 kilometres of trails make The Arboretum the perfect setting in which to search for insects such as dragonflies, damselflies and butterflies, while its many fruiting trees, shrubs and vines attract rare winter bird

↑ Thanks to a network of trails, visitors to the Arboretum have lots of opportunities to see at-risk trees and a variety of wildlife.

→ In fall, the mature fruit of the cucumber tree produces red fleshy pods containing scarlet seeds. Habitat loss has placed the tree on the endangered list.

species such as pine grosbeaks and Bohemian waxwings.

The Arboretum also has the oldest wildlife garden in Canada. The Gosling Wildlife Gardens displays five sample "backyards" that demonstrate how to attract wildlife to your property and provide them with food, water, shelter and space via ponds, recirculating streams, pollinator plants, trees, rock walls, restored forest, caterpillar plants, shelterbelts, fruiting shrubs and bird feeders.

Aylmer Wildlife Management Area

A massive migration spectacle

What Makes This Hot Spot Hot?

- Aylmer is a provincially significant wetland.
- Thousands of migrating tundra swans stop off every year.
- On-site observation decks make watching the spectacle easy.

Address: 10594 Hacienda Road, Aylmer, ON N5H 2R3
Swan line: (519) 773-7926
Website: naturallyelgin. com/natural-areas/aylmer-wildlife-management-area

Open year-round

↗ **Tundra swans head out on their epic migration.**

Southern Ontario really is a birder's dream spot. It has three of the Great Lakes, thousands of smaller lakes, large and small rivers, forest, wetland, field and scrubland. It is also on the boundary of the Carolinian Forest and the Great Lakes-St. Lawrence Forest Regions. Last but not least, major migration flyways are overhead. One species that stops here on its northward migration route is the tundra swan. And the best place to see these huge birds up close is the Alymer Wildlife Management Area.

Alymer is a 137-hectare area that served as a Royal Canadian Air Force base until 1961. Now it holds tallgrass prairie and a provincially significant wetland that attracts migrating waterfowl and shorebirds. If you're eager to see tundra swans, a visit in March will not disappoint. Eastern tundra

swans overwinter in Chesapeake Bay on the Atlantic Coast of the United States. Most of these birds fly more than 6,000 kilometres to reach their breeding grounds in the Mackenzie Delta in the Northwest Territories. While on this route, they typically stop only three times: once in southern Ontario, once in southern Manitoba/North Dakota and once in northern Alberta.

During their stop in southern Ontario, thousands wind up at Alymer, where they are fed corn to help fuel their journey. Alymer has observation platforms (including one that is wheelchair accessible) and volunteers to help you observe the swans and other waterfowl. The experience of seeing an expanse of these massive, white Arctic-bound birds should not be missed.

↑ An individual tundra swan preens its feather.

Backus Woods

Just north of Long Point, this tract of old-growth Carolinian forest is home to some of the oldest trees and rarest wildlife in Ontario

What Makes This Hot Spot Hot?

- Backus Wood holds some of the oldest Carolinian forest in Ontario, home to unusual and endangered tree species.
- Some of Ontario's rarest and most beautiful birds use the woods as breeding habitat.
- Well-groomed and accessible trails feature interpretive signage for visitors.

Address: 1267 Concession Road 4, Walsingham, ON N0E 1X0
Tel.: N/A
Website: natureconservancy.ca/en/where-we-work/ontario/featured-projects/backus-woods

Open year-round

↗ **The beauty of a male cerulean warbler is worth the patience it takes to find one high in the treetops.**

A step into Backus Woods, an hour south of Brantford, is a step into the past. Under the dense canopy of maple, oak and hickory, visitors can follow trails through lush forest, flooded sloughs and shrubby swamps. Birdsong rings through the trees, and rays of sunlight—filtered through the leaf-green lens above—dapple the forest floor. Forests like this once covered much of southern Ontario, but many were cleared for agriculture and development. Some trees here are hundreds of years old, and the oldest likely predate European settlement.

Over time, however, the forest that remains has not gone unchanged. American chestnut, once a dominant tree throughout southern Ontario, has largely disappeared due to disease. This endangered tree grows here in small numbers, and conservation efforts are underway to prevent its eradication. Other rare trees still thrive, including beautiful flowering dogwoods and towering tulip trees, the latter reaching

heights of over 35 metres.

The spectacular forest at Backus Woods also provides critical habitat for many uncommon birds. The endangered prothonotary warbler, one of Ontario's most brilliant birds, nests in swamps deep in the woods in fabricated boxes or natural tree cavities. Glimpses of its golden-yellow plumage can be caught as it forages in the understorey. Similarly endangered and equally striking cerulean warblers take a different approach, spending their time in the very tops of the trees to avoid being spotted. Watching these blue beauties requires good binoculars and strong neck muscles.

Owned by the Nature Conservancy of Canada, Backus Woods has 12 kilometres of trails that are open year-round. Interpretive signs introduce the visitor to the unique plants, animals and ecology of the forest. As the area is home to many sensitive species, care must be taken to stay on the trails to avoid disturbing habitat.

↑ **Sunlight filters through the leafy understorey at Backus Woods.**

Bannockburn Conservation Area

A small spot with a big message

What Makes This Hot Spot Hot?

- A natural island among agricultural fields, it is a magnet for local wildlife.
- It offers a living example of the ways in which landowners can enhance their properties and improve the environment.
- You can download a lovely educational audio tour of the site to your phone for a pleasant listening interlude during your hike.

Address: 76249 Bannockburn Line, Brucefield, ON N0M 1J0
Tel.: (519) 235–2610
(888)–286–2610
Website: abca.on.ca/page.php?page=bannockburn-conservation-area

Open year-round

At only 31 hectares, this tiny conservation area is an example of how even small natural spaces are important parts of Ontario's landscape. Surrounded by agricultural fields, Bannockburn Conservation Area showcases the ways in which landowners can enhance their own properties for wildlife. The area's boardwalks and bridges offer visitors access to wetlands, streams and the Bannockburn River, where rainbow trout or salmon can be seen making their way to spawning areas. These fish are still able to use the clear waters here because landowners upstream have protected the waterway by planting shade trees and shrubs along its banks to control erosion, filter pollutants and cool the water.

The mature forest at Bannockburn supports a variety of tree species. In summer, look for the alternate

branching and divided leaves of the bitternut hickory; in other seasons, look for the tree's distinctive yellow buds. Unfortunately, this species is currently infested with hickory bark beetle; some specimens have died and must be cut down. Once cut, the trunks are left on the ground; decaying plant matter provides nutrients for the forest as well as habitat for the small ground and soil dwellers of

❮ An American woodcock calls out.

➙ A wooden staircase leads up into the conservation area's mixed forest.

the area. Brush piles are left as hiding places for wildlife too.

The area's wet meadows provide a smorgasbord of food items for local birds—dogwood berries, weed seeds, hawthorn fruits and insects. The hawthorns, an early successional species, are also important nesting trees for American goldfinches and eastern kingbirds. On the ground, American woodcocks forage for worms and other soil invertebrates. Just before dark in early May, watch this bird's incredible flight display. Males sing a loud "peent" from the ground and then eventually take flight, ascending higher and higher in wide circles with twittering wings. When finally they can rise no farther, they drop earthward in a haphazard zigzag pattern, all the while issuing liquid chirping sounds before plopping to the ground and continuing their comical "peenting" calls.

Cedar Creek Conservation Area

Visit a vigorously protected piece of Carolinian Canada

What Makes This Hot Spot Hot?

- It's a unique opportunity to paddle through the heart of Carolinian Canada.
- You'll see examples of rare deciduous tree species.
- Birdwatchers can spot uncommon species living in a protected riparian habitat.

Address: County Road 23, Kingsville, ON
Tel.: (519) 776-5209
Website: erca.org/conservation-areas-events/conservation-areas/cedar-creek

Open year-round

At the extreme southern tip of southwestern Ontario, water helps define the landscape. Essex Region is bordered on three sides by the Detroit River, where the City of Windsor sits; Lake St. Clair, a freshwater lake that, with the Detroit River, plays an integral part in the Great Lakes system; and Lake Erie, the shallowest and warmest of the Great Lakes.

With its relatively mild climate, southerly location and proximity to the Great Lakes, Essex is the very heart of Carolinian Canada—it supports the greatest diversity of plants in the entire country. But as in the rest of southern Ontario, human activities over generations have dramatically reduced the historical forests and disrupted riparian vegetation. That's one of the reasons Cedar Creek is so treasured.

Thanks to the generosity of private landowners, the dedication of area residents and the guiding hand of the Essex Region Conservation

◄ A tulip tree's delicate bloom.

➔◄ Two views of the lush
Cedar Creek shoreline.

Authority, Cedar Creek is
regarded as one of the loveliest
natural areas in the region.
The creek itself flows into
Lake Erie, and along the way,
it and its tributaries are lined
with deciduous Carolinian
upland forest as well as rich
floodplain woods populated
by tree species such as the
tulip tree, sassafras, ironwood,
oaks, hickories and maples.
The springtime forest floor is a
sea of early wildflowers, from
trilliums and wild geraniums
to jack-in-the-pulpits and trout
lilies. Overhead along the
creek, eagles soar, and herons
and egrets wade at the water's
edge, as the rare American
lotus and swamp rose mallow
bloom. In fall, the deciduous
trees put on a vibrant show.

An ideal way to view the
area is by canoe or kayak
launched from the con-
servation area dock. An
hour-long paddle upstream
leads you through wetlands
and forests, where you will
enjoy a close-up view of
birds and other wildlife.

Devil's Punchbowl Conservation Area

A colourful slice of geological history in an increasingly densely populated part of the province

What Makes This Hot Spot Hot?

- This dramatic waterfall offers a vertical geology lesson.
- A visit to the Devil's Punchbowl is also a chance to hike some of the Bruce Trail.
- The surrounding area preserves rare communities of flora and fauna.

Address: Ridge Road, Stoney Creek, ON
Tel.: N/A
Website: waterfalls.hamilton.ca

Open year-round

🚶 🔭

↗ **During a hike at Devil's Punchbowl, you might see a yellow-billed cuckoo.**

The Niagara Escarpment is rightfully considered a treasure trove of natural wonders, and the Hamilton-area Devil's Punchbowl is, without question, one of these. Yet it might more accurately be described as a geological smorgasbord. The 100-metre-wide semicircular plunge pool at the foot of the Upper Falls was carved by massive meltwater at the end of the last ice age, and the exposed walls are a colourful composite of compressed sand, silt, clay and organic material from the ancient inland sea that covered the region.

Where glacial waters once roared, Stoney Creek now tamely meanders. From the parking lot, a small loop trail leads to a lookout platform. Also situated here is a 10-metre-tall steel cross. Some visitors to the Devil's Punchbowl Upper Falls may be a little disappointed, as the 37-metre-tall ribbon waterfall is often reduced to a mere trickle. But onlookers will appreciate the rare opportunity to take in this stratified slice of the escarpment's past, which spans over 40 million

years and shows the complete sequence from the Queenston Formation to the Lockport Formation. The Lower Falls, a charming six-metre classical waterfall, is located on the gorge below the lookout. (Visitors should be aware that there is no designated path to the smaller waterfall.)

Both waterfalls are located in the Devil's Punchbowl Conservation Area, a 42-hectare property that is managed by the Hamilton Conservation Authority. The Bruce Trail runs the length of the area, through red oak and white pine forest. The Niagara region is increasingly encroached upon by agricultural and suburban developments—all the more reason to enjoy a precious landscape that is renowned not only for its significant landforms but also for its diverse populations of plants, butterflies and birds.

↑ The Upper Falls at the Devil's Punchbowl Conservation Area drops 37 metres into a plunge pool.

Devonwood Conservation Area

A walk in an urban forest where a community of oaks fuels the cycle of life

What Makes This Hot Spot Hot?

- It's an opportunity to visit a protected area for trees and wildlife on the edge of town.
- Pop quiz: Can you identify the eight oak species that live here?
- If you look carefully, you might spy an owl perched deep in the forest.

Address: Division Road, Windsor, ON
Tel.: (519) 776-5209
Website: erca.org/conservation-areas-events/conservation-areas/devonwood

Open year-round

🚶 👓 🚴 ⛷️

↗ **An eastern screech-owl takes a snooze in a tree cavity.**

Windsor isn't New York City or Toronto, but every urban centre of a certain size deserves a natural getaway that goes beyond the bounds of a city park. On the outskirts of this most southwestern of Ontario cities, the Devonwood Conservation Area is such a destination.

Windsor sits on the southern shore of the Detroit River, where it enjoys a relatively moderate climate. Devonwood is a 38-hectare parcel of land that is characterized as a lowland clayplain forest. Oak is the dominant tree species here. Indeed, of some 10 different oak species that live in southern Ontario's Carolinian forest, eight grow in Devonwood—the red, white, black, swamp white, Chinquapin, pin, bur and Shumard oaks—probably a greater diversity of oaks than can be found anywhere else in the country. The oaks produce an abundance of "hard mast"—a crop of highly

nutritional acorns that provide a food source for wildlife, especially in winter. The white and swamp white oak, in particular, produce sweet, nutritional kernels that are sought after by birds and mammals once the cold weather sets in.

Some 4.5 kilometres of trail wind through the tranquil forest. The green canopy overhead creates more than enough privacy for the screech-owls and long-eared owls that make their home in this plant and wildlife sanctuary. Watch carefully, and you may spot one perched on a limb, almost but not quite obscured by tree branches and leaves.

↑ On a walk along the trails in Devonwood, look out for high-energy acorns from the Shumard oak strewn about on the forest floor.

↖↑ Keep your eye out for a Blackburnian warbler as you stroll the trails at Devonwood Conservation Area.

Elora Gorge Conservation Area

Explore this fast-flowing river on foot or by canoe, kayak or inner tube

What Makes This Hot Spot Hot?

- Enjoy a raging river bordered by tall cliffs.
- It's the perfect place to bring a wide-angle and/or fish-eye lens to capture the scenery.
- Visit the nearby 40-kilometre-long Elora-Cataract Trailway for a more extensive hiking or biking experience.

Address: 7400 Wellington County Road 21, Box 356 Elora, ON N0B 1S0
Tel.: (519) 846-9742
Website: grandriver.ca

Open May 1 to mid-October

↗ A close-up photograph of the gnarled roots of a white cedar makes a perfect piece of abstract art.

→ The Grand River in peaceful mode.

The 22-metre-high cliffs of the Elora Gorge in the Grand River valley near Guelph are sure to impress any newcomer to this small but dynamic conservation area. Opened in 1954, it was the first park established by the Grand River Conservation Authority. Now 200 hectares in size, this gorgeous park attracts more than 250,000 visitors a year.

As with so many other places in Ontario, this spot's beauty is a legacy of the meltwaters that surged through the region with the retreat of the glaciers in the last ice age. What is now the Grand River carved its way through limestone formed over 400 million years ago, when the area was covered by an inland sea. Made up of the remains of many generations of corals and molluscs, the gorge rock reveals just how significant a role that ancient sea played in building the current landscape.

As you hike the three-kilometre network of trails, keep an eye out for the organic artwork created by the roots of the northern white cedar. Sprawling over the ground and rocks, they inspire intriguing opportunities for abstract photography. One trail leads to the Hole in the Wall—just walk on through. Other trails follow the edge of the gorge and allow visitors to see the impressive view down to the river. Are you longing to experience the power of the river but don't have the canoe or kayak skills for this white water? At the Elora Gorge, you can rent inner tubes and safety equipment and ride the waves down the river and see for yourself how the gorge was formed. Erosion works!

Felker's Falls Conservation Area

A stunning terraced waterfall and upland woodlot just steps away from a residential area

What Makes This Hot Spot Hot?

- There's a vibrant waterfall just minutes from a suburban neighbourhood.
- Groomed trails lead visitors through one of the last remaining woodlots in the area.
- A careful observer might spot significant snakes by following the Bruce Trail through nearby fields.

Address: Ackland Street, Stoney Creek, ON L8J 1R3
Tel.: N/A
Website: waterfalls.hamilton.ca

Open year-round

The familiar sights of a suburban neighbourhood—playground equipment, privacy fences, parked cars—rarely include a full-fledged waterfall. Yet only a short walk from the Felker's Falls Conservation Area parking lot, a 22-metre terraced waterfall plunges over Davis Creek. With two main drops, Felker's Falls is notable not only for its beauty but also for its proximity to a residential neighbourhood between Hamilton and Stoney Creek.

Access points are offered from the Bruce Trail and from the Peter Street Trail, which allow you to walk both upstream and downstream through the creekside forest. As you walk upstream, note the smooth, bare spots along the creekbed, as well as the footbridge leading across the stream. Enjoy the vantage point from the other side as you walk back downstream. The gorge walls here are extremely steep, and visitors are advised to stay on the safe side of the fence.

Felker's Falls is one of several conservation areas characterized as "passive" by the Hamilton Conservation Authority (HCA), which manages all of them. The designation recognizes the

◄ Fallen trees span Davis Creek, downstream from the waterfall.

→ A terraced waterfall, Felker's Falls drops 22 metres in two stages.

central role each conservation area plays in the ecology and health of the HCA's watershed. As in so many developed areas, trees are among the first casualties, but a relatively undisturbed broadleaf upland woods continues to thrive on the slopes of the escarpment, establishing a critical connection between natural areas along the escarpment corridor. Beech, sugar maple and oak trees can be found in the woodlot, while the cliff edges are crowded with cedar and eastern hemlock.

The Bruce Trail runs along the top of the escarpment, offering an excellent view of the falls as well as a good view of Stoney Creek and Lake Ontario. The trail also passes through fields, with staghorn sumac and stands of bigtooth aspen punctuating the way. You might spot any of three locally significant snakes nestled in the grass: the red-bellied snake, the northern ringneck snake and the eastern smooth green snake.

Hawk Cliff

Eagles and falcons and hawks, oh my!

What Makes This Hot Spot Hot?

- Fifteen species of raptors regularly migrate past Hawk Cliff during the fall migration.
- On special weekends in September, bird banders show wild hawks to the public before the birds are released to continue their journey.
- When weather conditions aren't right for migrating raptors, visit nearby Fingal Wildlife Management Area and hike some of its 40 kilometres of trails.

Address: East of Port Stanley
Tel.: N/A
Website: ezlink.
ca/~thebrowns/HawkCliff

September and October are the best times to visit

While many of the northern Lake Erie shore birding sites are renowned for their spring migrations, fall is definitely the time to visit this hot spot. As the name suggests, at Hawk Cliff, hawks are the main event. Here, migrating raptors exploit uprisings of warm air known as thermals, riding them south and thereby conserving critical energy—these hunters can't always depend on feeding opportunities during the trip. Thermals don't form over water, so thousands of southbound raptors travel westward along the northern shore of Lake Ontario and Lake Erie as they search for a place where the water stops. That makes places like Hawk Cliff a sit-and-watch birding site; bring a lawn chair, and wait for the birds to come to you.

By deflecting southwest winds upward, the cliff itself provides another way for hawks to catch a ride. This air current is especially useful to peregrines, which can sometimes be seen coasting along the cliff edge at eye level, even on days when

migration traffic may be slow due to the absence of thermals. Osprey and eagles also like to take advantage of this uprising of air.

While hawk migration at Hawk Cliff can occur from August to December, mid-September is peak migration time for broad-winged hawks: The record for sightings in one day is an astonishing 130,000. Early October is the time to see the greatest variety of raptor species, when as many as 15 species in one day have been spotted.

Other birds are also held up

↑ A kettle of broad-winged hawks overhead at Hawk Cliff.

← View from the cliff.

by the daunting challenge of crossing the lake. As a result, you can often find warblers, flycatchers and vireos in the shrubs and trees near the cliff. As well, the presence of huge numbers of monarch butterflies and common green darner dragonflies provide ready evidence to observers that it isn't just the feathered that migrate south.

↑ A broad-winged hawk flying solo, shot from below.

Hillman Marsh Conservation Area

This marshland is for the birds, literally

What Makes This Hot Spot Hot?

- The Hillman Marsh offers intimate shorebird viewing opportunities.
- A carefully designed network of boardwalk trails allows visitors to explore a range of waterside habitats.
- Visit a handful of must-see natural areas within easy driving distance of the marsh.

Address: 1826 Mersea Road 2, Leamington, ON N8H 3V7
Tel.: (519) 776-5209
Website: erca.org/conservation-areas-events/conservation-areas/hillman-marsh

Open year-round

↗ **A late-summer view of the marsh from the boardwalk.**

→ **Though uncommon to Ontario, the marbled godwit has been spotted at Hillman Marsh.**

For a concentrated experience of marsh life, consider stopping off at this 344-hectare conservation area on the northern shore of Lake Erie. A mere minutes from Point Pelee National Park, the Hillman Marsh Conservation Area hosts an impressive 100-plus species during migration—from sandpipers, ducks and warblers to occasional visits from the yellow-headed blackbird, marbled godwit and yellow-crowned night-heron.

An array of habitats is home to diverse populations of shore, marsh and field birds at the marsh, where comfortable viewing opportunities have been designed for both serious birders and the simply curious. A two-hour stroll along a 4.5-kilometre trail around the wetland is time well spent in spring and summer and is guaranteed to inspire a future birder. Water levels at the specially devised 35-hectare shorebird habitat are intentionally managed to create mudflats during the spring migration season, vastly improving sight lines from the 2.7-kilometre shorebird trail that wraps around it.

At Hillman, the nature centre offers seasonal educational programs, including springtime interpretive displays about local flora and fauna. In May, the annual Spring Shore and Songbird Festival draws an enthusiastic audience. While you're in the area, take the opportunity to visit the nearby parks at Point Pelee and Wheatley. If you're keen to try out your land legs, a springtime hike through the Carolinian forest at Kopegaron Woods is a dream come true for naturalists and photographers.

Holiday Beach Conservation Area

Winged migration viewing at the end of Lake Erie

What Makes This Hot Spot Hot?

- *Audubon* magazine describes Holiday Beach as Canada's best hawk-watching spot and ranks it third overall in all of North America.
- Visitors can help researchers count migrating birds and insects.
- Visit during the Festival of Hawks events to come face-to-face with banded wild birds.

Address: 6952 County Rd 50, Amherstberg, ON N0R 1G0
Tel.: (519) 736-3772
Website: erca.org/conservation-areas-events/conservation-areas/holiday-beach

Open April to Thanksgiving

🚶 🔭 🚴 🛶 🏊 🎿 ⛺

↗ **Will this tagged monarch make it all the way to Mexico? Fingers crossed!**

On the shore of Lake Erie, Holiday Beach Conservation Area is a globally significant Important Bird Area (IBA) and home to the Holiday Beach Migration Observatory. The observatory has a three-storey observation tower to help visitors and researchers alike enjoy memorable sightings of migrating birds and insects—and there are lots of them to watch. In over 40 years, more than 3,000,000 hawks have been counted. Even daily totals can be impressive: Imagine counting 96,000 hawks, 600 hummingbirds, 250,000 blue jays or 10,000 cedar waxwings in just one day!

The observatory also bands birds and tags monarch butterflies. Monarchs that emerge from their chrysalises in Ontario in late August or

later are then likely to try to make the over 3,000-kilometre trek to their overwintering grounds in Mexico. But like migrating hawks, the monarchs prefer not to travel over large bodies of water if they don't have to. That's why Holiday Beach is such a great migration site: The migrating hawks and monarchs funnel their way to the site before they finally hop over the Detroit River and continue on their way south. At night, northern saw-whet owls migrate through Holiday Beach as well, and nocturnal researchers are able to catch and band them here. Banding these smallest of eastern North American owls is one of the only ways to learn about their migration patterns; unlike the easy-to-see, high-flying diurnal raptors, the nighttime movements of owls are difficult to observe.

Beside Holiday Beach is Big Creek Conservation Area. This huge wetland is part of the IBA and supports many water birds, including herons, egrets, ducks and geese. It can be viewed from the observatory at Holiday Beach.

↑ A northern saw-whet owl sports a new bird band.

↖ The blossoms of the aquatic American lotus cover the water at the nearby Big Creek wetland.

LaSalle Park

It's a birdwatching hot spot year-round, but to see the best of this urban oasis, you'll need to put on your parka

What Makes This Hot Spot Hot?

- LaSalle Park is home to some of the best winter waterfowl viewing in all of Ontario.
- This small tract of forest and ravine attracts many migrant songbirds in the spring and fall.
- Easily accessible from both Burlington and Hamilton, LaSalle is a perfect quick nature retreat.

Address: 501 Plains Road East, Burlington, ON L7T 2E7
Tel.: (905) 335-7738
Website: http://environmentaldefence.ca/issues/blue-flag-canada/map/lasalle-park-marina

Open year-round

↗ On the water in winter, a trumpeter swan and a bufflehead buddy.

Situated on the northern shore of Hamilton Harbour, 23-hectare LaSalle is a park with two identities. In the summer, it is an active marina, home to rows of yachts and cabin cruisers and bustling with locals and tourists alike. The winter, however, is a different story altogether.

Once the boats and docks are hauled out of LaSalle each fall, the warm, sheltered waters of the harbour attract waterfowl by the thousands. At least 20 species can be seen here regularly, with rarer types making occasional appearances. The convenient paths and close range make for exceptionally easy viewing that is perfect for the novice, casual observer or photographer.

In addition to the ducks, geese and swans that make LaSalle popular, uncommon birds like horned grebe and red-throated loon may be spotted diving in the open waters of the harbour. Bald eagles sometimes roost in trees nearby, and the breakwaters host a variety of gulls and the occasional visiting snowy owl.

While winter may be the

hottest season to visit LaSalle, don't neglect the spring and fall when the park's beautiful forests and ravines attract an array of migrating and resident songbirds. Carolinian specialties like the Carolina wren and the red-bellied woodpecker spend their year here, and numerous warblers, thrushes, vireos and others pass through on their way to warmer climes.

In any season, LaSalle Park's easy and free accessibility make it an ideal destination for a half an hour or half a day. With abundant birds and easy viewing, it is certain to impress not only naturalists but children and nature neophytes too.

↑ **Trumpeter swans, Canada geese and other waterfowl interact on the chilly waterfront at LaSalle Park.**

Long Point

Morning bird banding, a picnic lunch on the beach, an afternoon visit to the marsh and an evening search for an endangered toad

What Makes This Hot Spot Hot?

- Four hundred species of birds have been recorded in the Long Point area.
- There's an expansive marsh that attracts huge flocks of migrating waterfowl.
- Visitors can explore the area on foot, by bicycle, by canoe or by boat.

Address: Long Point Provincial Park, P.O. Box 99, 350 Erie Blvd Port Rowan, ON N0E 1M0
Tel.: (519) 586-2133
Websites: ontarioparks.com/park/longpoint; birdscanada.org/longpoint

Park grounds are open from mid-May to mid-October

➚ A sand-covered Fowler's toad might show itself to beachcombers during a nighttime stroll at Long Point.

A UNESCO World Biosphere Reserve, Long Point is a roughly 40-kilometre-long sand spit that juts out into Lake Erie from the lake's northern shore. One of the best places in Canada to watch birds, it is home to the Long Point National Wildlife Area, Long Point Provincial Park and the Long Point Bird Observatory. An important migration site, it and the surrounding region also provide vital nesting areas for over 175 species of birds.

This spot is home to a considerable number of species at risk, including the Fowler's toad. This endangered amphibian is in decline across Ontario, and Long Point is one of only three places where it still survives. Habitat degradation, vehicle use on beaches and pesticides are all implicated in its falling numbers. An evening hike along the over two kilometres

of sandy beach of Long Point Provincial Park may allow you to find and watch one of these rare amphibians, but be sure to not disturb it.

Just outside the provincial park entrance is the Old Cut Banding Station. This is part of the Long Point Bird Observatory, the oldest observatory of its kind in the Western Hemisphere. A morning visit to Old Cut during the spring (April and May) or fall (mid-August to early November) allows you to see first-hand how researchers catch and band birds. By re-catching birds that have already been previously banded, researchers gain a much more sophisticated understanding of the migration routes, physiological changes and population fluctuations of our birds. In 2014, Long Point Bird Observatory banded 26,683 birds from 166 species. Since it opened in 1960, it has banded 275 different bird species and almost one million individual birds.

↑ Banding little-known species such as the Connecticut warbler can reveal much to researchers.

↖ An aerial view of Long Point, a 40-kilometre sand spit that juts into Lake Erie.

Mosa Forest

Known locally by the colourful name 'Skunk's Misery,' Mosa Forest is one of the largest remaining tracts of Carolinian forest in southwestern Ontario

What Makes This Hot Spot Hot?

- In this incredibly diverse plant community, visitors can see many Carolinian species rarely observed elsewhere in Ontario.
- The forest is home to rare breeding birds such as the Acadian flycatcher, hooded warbler and yellow-billed cuckoo.
- It's a pristine tract of Carolinian forest that is "off the beaten track" and has few visitors.

Address: South side of Concession Drive, east of Sassafras Road, Southwest Middlesex
Tel.: (519) 354-7310
Websites: ontariotrails. on.ca/trails/view/mosa-forest-conservation-area-trail; Thames Talbot Land Trust: ttit.ca

Open year-round

↗ **The American chestnut leaf is identifiable by its length and the telltale teeth on its edge.**

Located halfway between London and Chatham-Kent, the lands that make up Mosa Forest are owned by the County of Middlesex, the Lower Thames Valley Conservation Authority and more than 50 private landowners. In total, 500 hectares of contiguous forest have been preserved, with adjacent swamp and tallgrass prairie completing a 1,200-hectare complex.

This remarkable Carolinian forest, swamp and prairie are home to over 700 different plants, including rare species such as American chestnut, black gum, flowering dogwood and sassafras. The unusual vegetation communities provide a home for equally unusual wildlife, and keen-eyed visitors might spot an eastern hog-nosed snake retreating into the grass or a southern flying squirrel gliding overhead. Even given these ecological strengths, however, "the Misery" is best known for its breeding birds.

Mosa Forest is one of the few places in Ontario in which Carolinian breeding specialties are found. In the

late spring and summer, visitors may hear the emphatic "peet-seet!" of the endangered Acadian flycatcher or the ringing "a-weet, a-weet, a-weet-ee-oh!" of the hooded warbler. Cryptic yellow-billed cuckoos skulk in the dense foliage, and blue-winged warblers can be seen flitting among the shrubs at the forest's edges. One of the forest's largest avian residents—the pileated woodpecker—can frequently be heard drumming on trees in search of concealed insects.

Experiencing all that Mosa Forest has to offer requires an adventurous spirit and a can of your favourite bug repellent, as the mosquito population is always thriving. The forest is accessible from the rectangle formed by Dogwood Road, Centreville Drive, Sassafras Road and Concession Drive. Reasonable trails enter the forest from the roadside, but care must be taken to stay on established trails at all times to avoid damaging sensitive vegetation communities. For those brave enough to explore it, Skunk's Misery has a wealth of treasures just waiting to be discovered.

↑ **An aerial view of Mosa Forest, a.k.a., Skunk's Misery.**

Mount Nemo Conservation Area

Soaring with the raptors

What Makes This Hot Spot Hot?

- At the cliff edge, there are incredible 50-kilometre views.
- A scattering of large boulders and rock fissures add to the site's ruggedness.
- Watch raptors such as soaring turkey vultures and red-tailed hawks from above.

Address: 5317 Guelph Line Burlington, ON L9T 2X6
Tel.: (905) 854-0262
Websites: conservationhalton.ca/mount-nemo; brucetrail.org

Open year-round

From the cliff top at the Mount Nemo Conservation Area, visitors can enjoy stunning panoramic views of the Niagara Escarpment and the surrounding countryside. If the sky is clear, it's even possible to see the CN tower from here. In short, it's a beautiful place to see other beautiful places.

A hiker's paradise, Mount Nemo, which is located on the outskirts of Burlington, roughly halfway along the Niagara Escarpment, has two trails. The 2.3-kilometre North Loop Trail and the 2.6-kilometre South Loop Trail range in difficulty from beginner to intermediate and can be hiked in an hour and an hour and a quarter respectively. These trails link into Canada's oldest and longest marked hiking trail—at some 890 kilometres, the Bruce Trail stretches from the Niagara region to Tobermory, at the tip of the Bruce Peninsula. It's at the top of every serious hiker's must-do list, whether travelled in its entirety over a month or so or done in sections over several seasons.

Mount Nemo's cliff ecosystem is renowned on the Niagara Escarpment. Limestone boulders are cloaked in ferns and mosses throughout the old-growth forest, while the trail that winds along the cliff edge offers a glimpse of crevice caves and the 1,000-year-old cedars that eke out a living here. From the impressive cliff edge, you'll appreciate an unusual birdwatching perspective—at this height, you're on the same level as the soaring turkey vultures. The most commonly seen species at Mount Nemo, this raptor is a graceful flier, but it is also enjoys an advantage—unlike most birds, the turkey vulture has an incredible sense of smell. It is able to detect an animal carcass from a distance of hundreds of metres even if it is concealed by trees at the bottom of the cliff. When the turkey vulture drops to the ground to feed on its carrion prey, you can actually birdwatch *from above*.

↑ A turkey vulture on the hunt for a meal of carrion.

↖ Visitors enjoy a big view of the surrounding countryside from Mount Nemo.

← Cedar trees stubbornly gain purchase on the rocky limestone slope.

Mountsberg Conservation Area

A nature experience for all ages and interests

What Makes This Hot Spot Hot?

- The Mountsberg reservoir is a haven for wetland species, including the bald eagle, osprey, great blue heron, wood duck, muskrat and many species of dragonfly.
- At the Raptor Centre, nose-to-beak live bird demonstrations teach you more about hawks and owls.
- Kids can visit a maple syrup town and learn about the process that turns sweet sap into syrup.

Address: 2259 Milburough Line Campbellville, ON L0P 1B0
Tel.: (905) 854-2276
Website: conservationhalton. ca/mountsberg

Open year-round

↗ **An osprey delivers building material for its stick nest.**

If you're searching for a weekend nature outing in early spring that everyone in the family is sure to enjoy, Mountsberg Conservation Area is the place. First on the menu—something gastronomic. Mountsberg's amazing maple syrup program starts with a horse-drawn wagon ride and wraps up with an irresistible stack of pancakes smothered in homemade maple syrup. In between, learn why sugar and black maples are the trees of choice for Canada's most famous food and how the syrup is made. While in the sugar bush, watch for black-capped chickadees and listen for drumming ruffed grouse.

Visit the Raptor Centre to find out more about your favourite meat-eating birds. Demonstrations with educational raptors offer tips on identification, breeding

biology, hunting techniques and conservation strategies for hawks, owls, falcons, eagles and vultures. Then, hike to the edge of the huge reservoir and try your luck at spotting a wild bald eagle perched in a tree or an osprey grabbing a stick to add to its growing nest. Scan the water surface for ducks of various species as well as swallows, sparrows, blackbirds and herons.

For an even more interactive experience, sign up for one of Mountsberg's famous owl prowls. Meet the live educational owls before heading out into the night woods to call out to wild great horned owls and eastern screech-owls: They may very well call back. Other nature experiences at Mountsberg include exploring a pond, taking a nature hike or visiting the captive bison herd.

↑ The sugar maples burst into fall colour at Mountsberg.

Ojibway Nature Centre's Ojibway Prairie Complex

A rare ecosystem that supports plant and animal species scarcely found anywhere else in the province

What Makes This Hot Spot Hot?

- Ojibway Prairie Complex represents one of Ontario's largest remaining tracts of tall-grass prairie.
- The 350-hectare complex is home to plant and animal species that are found in very few places in Ontario.
- The site is easily accessible via a beautiful nature centre with friendly, knowledgeable staff.

Address: 5200 Matchette Road, Windsor, ON N9C 4E8
Tel.: (519) 966-5852
Website: ojibway.ca

Open year-round

🚶 🔭

↗ **Prairie wildflowers in bloom at Ojibway.**

→ **A skilled climber, the fox snake can often be found wrapped around a tree branch rather than on the ground.**

Located just a few kilometres from downtown Windsor, in Ontario's extreme southwestern corner, the Ojibway Prairie Complex is a collection of five natural areas that protect some of the province's best examples of tallgrass prairie. An ecosystem that supports significant biodiversity, the tallgrass prairie has made this site a one-of-a-kind refuge for plants and animals that live in few other parts of Ontario.

Tallgrass prairie once covered more than 40,000 hectares of southern Ontario, but over time, as a result of decades of agricultural encroachment and tree removal, only small remnants survive. Prairie wildflowers are among the most beautiful in Ontario, and many rare species grow here, including the showy, dense blazing-star and delicate eastern prairie white-fringed orchid. Flowers bloom from spring through fall, and there is no bad time to see their impressive display.

Unusual wildlife inhabits the prairie too. Ojibway is one of few places in Ontario where the endangered eastern fox snake and the Butler's garter snake can be spotted gliding through the grasses. More than 90 species of butterflies and skippers feed on the wildflowers here, and dozens of species of dragonflies and damselflies forage over the paths and ponds. Carolinian birds such as the tufted titmouse and the red-bellied woodpecker regularly visit the birdfeeders, and the eastern screech-owl can often be seen near the Ojibway Nature Centre.

The Prairie Complex is best accessed from the Ojibway Nature Centre itself, where knowledgeable staff can help

you plan your visit. Beautiful displays in the centre provide a preview of what may be encountered in the complex. Well-groomed trails—some of which are stroller and wheel-chair accessible—take the visitor through prairie, savannah and woodland, while wildflower gardens and ponds near the building allow excellent viewing opportunities with less walking. The centre is open every day, and admission and parking are free of charge.

Old Ausable Channel

Creating a natural-succession plan for an orphaned waterway in the centre of a provincial park

What Makes This Hot Spot Hot?

- Part river, part pond, the OAC sustains an unusual constellation of aquatic flora and fauna but faces an uncertain future.
- The channel flows through a rare oak savannah community.
- The watershed is home to an abundance of wildlife.

Address: Pinery Provincial Park, 9526 Lakeshore Road, Hwy 21, Grand Bend, ON N0M 1T0
Tel.: (519) 243-2220
Website: oldausablechannel.ca

Open year-round

↗ **Once part of the Ausable River, the Old Ausable Channel is now considered a tributary.**

It wouldn't be wrong to call the Old Ausable Channel (OAC) an accident of history. Originating in the moraines near the village of Staffa, the Ausable River once flowed north to Grand Bend before abruptly sweeping south in a "grand bend" to its outlet at Port Franks. In the late 19th century, as a remedy for area flooding, the river was cut and rerouted, then cut again to create a harbour at Grand Bend. As a result, this 14-kilometre section of the Ausable River was effectively orphaned. With no access to water from upstream sources, the OAC is a warm-water, low-flow system that is fed entirely by precipitation, springs and a modest amount of surface runoff. At its southern end, a dam maintains water levels in the channel before it flows into the present-day Ausable River Cut at Port Franks.

Characterized by clear water with dense aquatic vegetation above the dam, the channel is a unique ecosystem. The balance of the OAC runs through Pinery Provincial Park, where it is part of the Dunes watershed, which boasts a rare oak savannah community and provincially significant flora,

such as the yellow puccoon. Butterfly milkweed, blazing star and poke milkweed also thrive here, as do a range of shade-tolerant wildflowers. The channel is home to a diverse fish community; three species at risk are found here: the pugnose shiner, the lake chubsucker and the grass pickerel. Paddlers can explore the peaceful waterway, watching for native plant species, including swamp rose, buttonbush and wild calla, as well as a host of small mammals, reptiles, birds and butterflies.

Cut off from the rest of the river, however, the OAC is almost certainly destined to eventually convert from an aquatic ecosystem to a more terrestrial ecosystem over many years of natural succession. The challenge for the Ausable Bayfield Conservation Authority and other regional stakeholders is to manage that evolution in a way that respects the inexorable forces of nature. An invaluable natural habitat depends on it.

↑ **A view from an OAC lookout over the wetland.**

Pelee Island

Rare species and a wine tour make a visit to this southern Canadian island one the whole family can enjoy

What Makes This Hot Spot Hot?

- A ferry ride takes you to a must-visit destination for every Ontario naturalist.
- Rare plants and animals are found throughout the island.
- The promise of a wine tour is sure to entice a non-nature-obsessed spouse or partner to make the trip with you.

Address: For information about travelling to Pelee Island by ferry, visit pelee. org/tourism/getting-here
Tel.: N/A
Websites: ontarionature. org/protect/habitat/stone_ road_alvar.php; pelee.com/ lighthouse-point-provincial-nature-reserve/; pelee.com/fish-point-provincial-nature-reserve

Ferry runs from late March to early December (book ahead)

Pelee Island's prime location at the very southern edge of Canada has significant consequences for this large island's native plant and animal residents. Thanks to its southerly position and the moderating effect of western Lake Erie, the island enjoys a milder climate than nearby mainland areas. As a result, several natural areas on the island are able to support a plethora of rare species that would struggle to survive elsewhere.

One of these, the 42-hectare Stone Road Alvar Nature Reserve, protects 44 provincially rare and 33 regionally rare plants. These plants have adapted to the globally rare alvar habitat, which is made up of limestone plains that can become extremely hot in the summer months. Some species, such as the downy wood mint, are found only on Pelee Island and nowhere else in Canada. Provincially rare trees that grow here include the Chinquapin oak, hop tree and blue ash.

The island is also on an important flyway for migrating birds. Fish Point Provincial Nature Reserve and

◀ Meet the blue racer: Pelee Island holds the only Canadian population.

→ The lighthouse at Lighthouse Point, built in 1833.

Lighthouse Point Provincial Nature Reserve are birding hot spots where spring migrants sometimes gather in species-diverse flocks during their northward travels. These and other natural areas on the island are home to many rare reptiles and amphibians, including the Lake Erie water snake, eastern fox snake and eastern spiny softshell turtle. The blue racer, a gorgeous steel-grey snake, and the smallmouth salamander are found nowhere else in Canada.

If you have a partner or friend who is less of a nature geek than you are, Pelee Island is the perfect spot. Promise a refreshing ferry ride, a wine tour and a stay in one of the island's many bed and breakfasts. While touring around the island, keep your eyes out for a grey fox. This small canine is partially arboreal and relatively adept at climbing trees for a member of the dog family. Though uncommon, one just might appear during your visit.

Pinery Provincial Park

Southwestern Ontario's super park

What Makes This Hot Spot Hot?

- Visitors can find some of Canada's most endangered plants and animals here.
- Pinery is the meeting place of oak savannah and freshwater coastal dune habitats.
- Finding and photographing a rare insect is a good possibility.

Address: 9526 Lakeshore Road, Grand Bend, ON N0M 1T0
Tel.: (519) 243-2220
Websites: ontarioparks.com/park/pinery; pinerypark.on.ca

Open year-round

↗ **Habitat has put the strikingly beautiful red-headed woodpecker on the threatened list.**

Pinery has it all: a rare forest type, a river channel, a Great Lake shoreline and endangered wildlife species—all contained in an area that spans 2,532 hectares. Established as a provincial park in 1959, Pinery today preserves almost half of the world's remaining oak savannah, defined as a transition community between an open prairie grassland and a canopy-covered oak forest. This zone survives best when periodic fires suppress a variety of tree species but allow fire-tolerant oaks to survive. When Europeans arrived in this area, their method of land stewardship was to transform the savannahs into farmland and to smother these important fires. Both approaches critically altered the habitat's vital community structure. The remnant oak savannah here is now managed through prescribed burns to ensure the survivability of this rare space and all its plant and animal inhabitants.

Freshwater coastal dunes are another intriguing park habitat. These sandy ridges support a number of plants that are adapted to the site's extreme conditions, from freezing winter weather to summer ground-level temperatures that can reach a sizzling 70 degrees C. Dune grasses help hold this habitat together, so it's especially important that visitors stay on the marked trails.

Pinery is an important bird migration stopover site

for everything from swans to sparrows. Breeding birds abound here too, including rare ones such as the piping plover (endangered), red-headed woodpecker (threatened), cerulean warbler (endangered) and Louisiana waterthrush (special concern). Another animal group that makes Pinery very special is insects. Some Canadian firsts found here include a damselfly and a rhinoceros beetle and many species of moths and ants. It is also home to a globally rare tiger beetle. And keep your eye peeled for the rusty-patched bumble bee. Once the fourth most common bumble bee in southwestern Ontario, this insect is now endangered, and Pinery is the only place in Ontario where this species has been seen since 2002. That's just additional proof that this park is a special place for nature as well as for naturalists.

↑ **A boardwalk leads over the dunes to Lake Huron.**

Point Pelee National Park

You'll find North America's best inland bird migration site at the southernmost tip of mainland Canada

What Makes This Hot Spot Hot?

- Birders from all over the world come here to see the spring migration.
- Point Pelee has been dubbed the "Warbler capital of North America": The record number of warbler species seen by an individual birder in one day is 34.
- Walk to the tip and become the southernmost mainland citizen of Canada.

Address: 1118 Point Pelee Drive Leamington, ON N8H 3V4
Tel.: 519-322-2365
Website: pc.gc.ca/eng/pn-np/on/pelee/index.aspx

Park grounds are open year-round

↗ **The sweet-singing American redstart breeds at Point Pelee. Hopping from branch to branch, this warbler uses its dramatic colour to startle its insect prey into the open.**

→ **Watch for turtles and fish from the marsh boardwalk.**

If you want to see birds during spring migration, this is the spot. Vireos, flycatchers, orioles, sparrows, warblers—they're all here. Mid-May is Point Pelee's peak time for both birds and birders, and while it can be busy, the human population density also makes it a great spot for beginners to get help. Most birders are only too willing to fill in newbies on the habits of that difficult vireo sitting overhead or to identify the strange song coming from the shrubs.

Point Pelee is a great spring migration spot largely because of its long southern reach into Lake Erie. Most small birds are nocturnal migrants and may fly hundreds of kilometres in one night. If they're still over the lake once morning comes, they have no choice but to continue flying until they reach land. Point Pelee might be the first spot they see, and that fact funnels many birds into the park's beach, forest, savannah, swamp and marsh habitats.

But Point Pelee isn't only

about birds. You may find an endangered eastern fox snake sunning itself on the side of a trail, a brilliant yellow hairy puccoon in full bloom near the beach or a juniper hairstreak butterfly sitting on an eastern red cedar. And don't miss the marsh boardwalk. It's an excellent place to watch for turtles, and a short walk might turn up snapping, northern map, painted and Blanding's turtles taking a break in the sun. You may also see some of the marsh's fish life as you gaze into the water—perhaps a long-time park denizen such as the spotted gar, a primitive ray-finned fish whose family has made North America home for the past 100 million years.

Rock Glen Conservation Area

A hike along a riverbed turns up clues about life on Earth 350 million years ago

What Makes This Hot Spot Hot?

- It's a transition zone between two forest types.
- Rock Glen is one of the best repositories of Middle Devonian Era fossils on the continent.
- The area is a rich source of indigenous artifacts.

Address: 8680 Rock Glen Road, Arkona, ON N0M 1B0
Tel.: (519) 828-3071
Website: abca.on.ca

Open year-round, weather permitting

↗ **Stop by at the Arkona Lions Museum and Information Centre to learn more about the area's rich store of fossils.**

It's not often that human and geological history, physical beauty, biodiversity and family fun come together in one place, but you can find it all at the 27-hectare Rock Glen Conservation Area, just outside the village of Arkona.

Located in the transition zone between the Carolinian Forest Region and the Great Lakes–St. Lawrence Lowlands, Rock Glen is home to an abundance of tree species from each area, from the heat-loving sycamore, sassafras and tulip tree to familiar cold-hardy species such as the sugar maple, beech, white elm and basswood. As many as 50 species of wildflowers burst into bloom each spring, as the sounds of songbirds fill the air and small mammals scurry through the underbrush. If that weren't enough, there are playgrounds, trails, boardwalks, a scenic lookout and a lovely 10.7-metre waterfall on Rock Glen Creek that cascades into a pool at its base.

But perhaps Rock Glen's most compelling aspect is tied to what it was some 350 million years ago. In place of a stand of deciduous trees and a rushing river, imagine a shallow sea, teeming with millions of hard-shelled marine

animals known as brachiopods, filter-feeding echinoderms named crinoids, horn corals and three-lobed arthropods. As the sea retreated, these creatures were buried in ocean-floor sediment. The result? Layer upon layer of sedimentary rock studded with clues about the Earth's history, obscured for millennia by a glacier and then a lake. Thanks to an earthquake that split the bedrock 10,000 years ago, these fossils were exposed. Today, Rock Glen is one of the best repositories of Middle Devonian Era fossils in North America, as well as a productive site for artifacts from the Early and Archaic First Nations people who made their living in the area hunting barren ground caribou.

Although you are not allowed to dig for them, heavy rains often free fossils embedded in the walls of the river gorge, washing them down to the streambed. Excited would-be geologists are allowed to take one sample with them when they leave.

The whole family can learn more about the area's human and geological history at the on-site Arkona Lions Museum and Information Centre.

⊤ **The cascading waterfall on Rock Glen Creek is the area's scenic centrepiece.**

Rockwood Conservation Area

A bit of the north right here in the south

What Makes This Hot Spot Hot?

- It's a geological hot spot with cliffs and potholes.
- You can visit the picturesque ruins of an old stone woolen mill.
- Be brave—crawl through a cave.

Address: 161 Fall Street
Rockwood, ON N0B 2K0
Tel.: (519) 856-9543
Website: grandriver.
ca/index/document.
cfm?Sec=27&Sub1=130&sub2=0

Open May 1 to mid-October

⬈ One of the largest forest birds in North America, the pileated woodpecker can be heard—and sometimes seen—pounding on trees and fallen branches in search of its favourite prey, carpenter ants.

Rockwood Conservation Area is a small space with a great big personality. Here, dramatic limestone cliffs overgrown with mixed forest border a small lake and river edges. It's hard not to feel that someone has carved out a piece of the Bruce Peninsula and plopped it into southern Ontario. The corresponding trails feature steep and flat sections that take you along both sides of the Eramosa River and lake areas. The area's limestone geology and past glaciation has also resulted in some of Ontario's best caves—there are 12 in all, many of which can be explored by the adventurous visitor.

Perhaps a more accessible geological wonder is Rockwood's more than 200 potholes, also known as kettles. These circular pits were formed by meltwater that ran under or beside the retreating glacier some 13,000 to 12,000 years ago. The flowing water picked up fist-sized rocks, which circled in eddies, grinding large circular holes into the limestone (which is not limestone at all but a sedimentary cousin known as a crystalline dolostone). Several of these potholes are easily visible from a boardwalk near the edge of the lake. Partially filled with water, they create pond-like habitats for creatures such as the larvae of blue-spotted salamanders.

Other watery sections of the Rockwood Conservation Area are wonderful places to study aquatic organisms. A dip net and an old pair of running shoes are all you need to explore this underwater world. A few scoops in the

↑ A view of a northern Ontario landscape, right here in southern Ontario.

→ An artifact of retreating glacial meltwaters, the Rockwood potholes create a miniature pond-like habitat.

river sections should turn up the nymphs of mayflies, dragonflies, damselflies and stoneflies as well as crayfish and darters. Above the water, Rockwood Conservation Area is a wonderful place to see a pileated woodpecker. These impressive birds seem to be quite comfortable around visitors and can occasionally be watched at very close range.

Rondeau Provincial Park

Large Carolinian trees, extensive wetlands and the best spot in Canada to see the brilliant prothonotary warbler

What Makes This Hot Spot Hot?

- Rondeau's trail systems extend through a variety of different habitats, including oak savannah, Carolinian forest, swamp, marsh and coastal dunes.
- There are towering old-growth tulip trees.
- More at-risk species are found here than in any other Ontario provincial park.

Address: 18050 Rondeau Park Road, Morpeth, ON N0P 1X0
Tel.: (519) 674-1750
Website: ontarioparks.com/park/rondeau

Open year-round

↗ **Rondeau is renowned for its population of eye-catching prothonotary warblers.**

→ **The tulip tree reaches heights of up to 50 metres and can be readily identified by its distinct four-lobed leaves and tulip-like flowers.**

The second oldest of Ontario's provincial parks, Rondeau Provincial Park was founded in 1894. Its early designation may be the reason that the park still boasts one of the largest tracts of extant Carolinian forest in Canada. A sand spit that juts into Lake Erie in a crescent shape that forms a circular bay, the park bears a French name meaning "round water." Varied habitats and southern location make Rondeau an important area for Canadian species at risk—fauna that includes the five-lined skink, eastern hog-nosed snake and acadian flycatcher, and flora such as the red mulberry, swamp rose-mallow, nodding pogonia and broad beech fern.

Another at-risk species found here is the endangered prothonotary warbler. Rondeau harbours Canada's largest breeding population of this species. It is one of our largest warblers, and its golden plumage almost glows as you watch it forage in its swampy

habitat. It's the only one of our warbler species to nest in cavities, and if you wait patiently and quietly from a forested boardwalk trail, you may be lucky enough to see one enter a nest box or a hole in a stump.

In addition to its over 10 kilometres of beaches, Rondeau has a variety of trail systems that offer plenty of exploring opportunities during spring and fall migration. Bring your binoculars, as over 330 bird species have been recorded here. Your plant field guides will come in handy as well, because the diversity of both woody and flowering plants in the park is truly astounding.

Royal Botanical Gardens

'Canada's Biodiversity Hot Spot'—a natural jewel just outside of the GTA

What Makes This Hot Spot Hot?

- RBG is home to a staggering diversity of plants, fish, birds and other wildlife.
- This tract of Carolinian forest is among the northernmost in Ontario and the most accessible from the GTA.
- RBG's natural areas range from escarpment bluffs to lowland marshes and offer incredible scenery and diverse habitats.

Address: 680 Plains Road West, Burlington, ON L7T 4H4
Tel.: (905) 527-1158
Website: rbg.ca

Open year-round

↗ **There are excellent birding opportunities along Caleb's Walk, one of the many trails at RBG.**

Royal Botanical Gardens (RBG) gained early attention in the 1930s as the Hamilton region's first botanical garden, inspired by England's illustrious Kew Gardens. Today, RBG protects more than 900 hectares of stunning nature sanctuaries, with features that include escarpment bluffs, Carolinian forest, cutting ravines, scenic creeks and an expansive marsh. A migratory bird stopover and a plant biodiversity hot spot, it also has one of the largest fish hatcheries on Lake Ontario.

Royal Botanical Gardens consists of three main areas. Adjacent to RBG Centre is Hendrie Valley—a picturesque wetland complex centred on Grindstone Creek. The creek and floodplain marshes host spawning fish such as salmon and pike, while wood ducks and other waterfowl raise their young among the vegetation. A carefully monitored population of threatened Blanding's turtles live here, and boardwalks and smooth trails make this a great nature-walk destination for the whole family.

Cootes Paradise is an enormous river-mouth marsh,

once destroyed by human activity but now on the road to restoration. The marsh provides excellent seasonal waterfowl viewing, and in 2013 was home to the first successful bald eagle nest on the Canadian shore of Lake Ontario in over 50 years. Trails follow both the northern and southern shores, winding through glacial ravines and over burbling creeks. In 1997, The Fishway was opened, an innovation that blocks the entry of invasive carp into Cootes Paradise while allowing dozens of native fish species into the marsh to breed.

The remote Rock Chapel and Berry Tract provide access to spectacular escarpment scenery. Cliff lookouts and nearby Borer's Falls present photo opportunities, while spring wildflowers and fall colours create dazzling seasonal displays. The keen observer may spot a red mulberry—more examples of this endangered tree are found here than anywhere else in Canada.

Nestled among the most urban parts of Ontario, RBG is an oasis for the nature lover. Visit in any season, and its natural riches will not disappoint.

↑ Fruit from the red mulberry, an endangered tree that thrives at the RBG.

↖ A lookout over Cootes Paradise, complete with binoculars and interpretive signage.

Saint Clair National Wildlife Area

A mighty migration marsh

What Makes This Hot Spot Hot?

- On major flyway routes, Saint Clair is an extensive marsh that attracts migrating waterfowl.
- Many marsh animals live and raise their young here.
- Saint Clair is home to 20 at-risk animal and plant species.

Address: Pain Court, ON N0P 1Z0
Tel.: Environment Canada @ (800) 668-6767
Website: ec.gc.ca/ap-pa/default.asp?n=9320E848-1

Open year-round

➤ This wildlife area is one of the best places in Ontario to see the secretive least bittern, one of the smallest herons in the world.

Saint Clair National Wildlife Area, just west of Chatham, is such an important waterfowl stopover site that it has been designated a Ramsar wetland of international importance. Hundreds of thousands of ducks, geese and swans stop here every spring and fall. To better protect these birds, much of the area has restricted access, but a trail and viewing tower are open for wildlife watching. It's also possible to see and photograph wildlife from the roads.

One of the smallest herons in the world, the least bittern is extremely adept at blending into its cattail home at Saint Clair, which is one of the best places in Ontario to see it. Another species found in the watershed area that feeds the marsh is the queen snake. This aquatic snake happens to be a very picky eater with special dietary requirements—it typically eats only crayfish. And not just regular crayfish; it prefers freshly moulted specimens. There are also small, remnant patches of tallgrass prairie here that attract terrestrial animals, including many species of butterfly. Great numbers of southbound monarchs stop at Saint Clair and, as a result, this spot has been named an International Butterfly Reserve.

Most of the reserve, however,

is made up of cattail marsh. Cattails are adapted to spread quickly in wet areas through vegetative reproduction by rhizomes and by seeds that are transported on the wind. They provide a home for marsh animals such as the northern harrier, swamp sparrow, marsh wren, common yellowthroat, common gallinule, American coot, muskrat, mink and many species of turtles, snakes and frogs. Unfortunately, many of Ontario's marshes, including Saint Clair, are currently under threat by non-native *Phragmites*, an invasive common reed that disturbs the ecological health of our wetlands by outcompeting the native cattails. Researchers are hard at work developing strategies to control this aggressive species at Ontario wetland habitats.

↑ **A view of the marsh in early winter.**

St. Williams Conservation Reserve

Celebrating more than a century of forest restoration and management in Ontario

What Makes This Hot Spot Hot?

- It's a biodiversity centre with a host of rare species, from the bird's-foot violet and American chestnut to the hooded warbler, Acadian flycatcher and eastern whip-poor-will.
- The area has a rich history of forest management and restoration.
- The multiuse trails include opportunities for hiking, mountain biking and horseback riding.

Address: Ministry of Natural Resources/Aylmer District, 615 John Street North, Aylmer, ON N5H 2S8
Tel.: (519) 773-9241
Website: swcr.ca

Open year-round

🚶 👓 🚴 ⛷

↗ **The fabulous blooms of the endangered eastern flowering dogwood.**

The St. Williams Conservation Reserve is part of the Norfolk Sand Plain, a delta that formed on the northern shore of Lake Erie after the retreat of the last ice age's glaciers. Early pioneers eventually settled much of this land, clear-cutting populations of native trees and plants over time and exposing the sandy soil to the elements. The St. Williams Forestry Project was established more than a century ago to grow and plant seedlings in an effort to stabilize what had effectively become desert areas. As one of the first projects in Canada, it serves as a model for subsequent initiatives.

Made up of oak woodland, oak savannah, forest, wetlands and sand barrens, the St. Williams Conservation Reserve is located on Crown land within the Long Point Biosphere Preserve. With

more than 1,000 hectares at two sites, the reserve is a multiuse area that supports a great number of Canadian species at risk. Today, it is is being managed to restore and preserve the richly diverse Carolinian habitats and flora and fauna populations that once flourished here.

While exploring the trails,

keep your eye open for one of Ontario's most beautiful and endangered woody plants, the eastern flowering dogwood. This small tree is alive with large blooms in May. Interestingly, the white "petals" on the four-parted flowers are not petals at all but bracts, a leaf-like structure that has taken on the petal's job of attracting pollinators with their showy colour. The familiar poinsettia and bougainvillea plants share the same characteristic.

Another St. Williams denizen to watch for is the eastern hog-nosed snake, our most "dramatic" serpent. When attacked, it hisses, makes a striking motion, flattens its neck and even plays dead. It's all part of a harmless yet theatrical display intended to discourage a potential predator. Unfortunately, in recent years, this snake has moved from threatening to

threatened as its population has declined; a research project at St. Williams is focused on how to preserve this intriguing Ontario species.

↑ Look but don't touch. The larva of an Io moth, found at St. Williams, is covered with spines that sting.

↓ A young eastern hog-nosed snake does its best to look threatening.

Thames Valley Trail

This river trail allows you to explore nature in the rural countryside and in the heart of a large city

What Makes This Hot Spot Hot?

- Hikers can follow a major river through Canada's Carolinian forests.
- Visitors enjoy nature in an easily accessible urban setting.
- Contact the Thames Valley Trail Association to learn more about its year-round guided hikes.

Address: Thames Valley Trail Association, Inc. c/o Grosvenor Lodge, 1017 Western Road, London ON N6G 1G5
Tel.: (519)-645-2845
Website: tvta.ca

Open year-round. Note: Some sections may flood in early spring and late fall.

The Thames Valley Trail follows a meandering 130-kilometre path along the Thames River, one of southern Ontario's major waterways. The river's three main branches—known today as the North, Middle and South Thames—inspired the Odawa and Ojibwe to name it the "Antlered River." The trail follows these branches through diverse habitats in the Carolinian Forest Region, in which a wide range of plant species thrive. In spring, populations of trilliums and other wildflowers explode in the forests, while the pungent smell of early-blooming skunk cabbage permeates the air in swampy wetlands. In open areas, you'll find everything from meadow herbs to cultivated crops.

The North Branch and South Branch meet at The Forks in the heart of the City of London, and flow through downtown parks. Thanks to these green spaces, urban wildlife, from rabbits and groundhogs to white-tailed deer and coyotes, flourish. While parts of the Thames here are lined with concrete embankments, the vantage points from the raised trail allow naturalists to watch for aquatic

⬐ The eastern spiny softshell turtle can be found along the banks of the Thames River.

→ The long, meandering Thames Valley Trail traces the path of the river through downtown London, Ontario.

wildlife—you might spy a cormorant or a family of mink fishing underwater. Watching overhead has its rewards as well. Osprey nest on the local light standards, bald eagles patrol the river, and red-tailed hawks perch in the park trees.

The sight of an eastern spiny softshell turtle sunning itself along the muddy banks is a special treat. With its pancake-shaped leathery shell and long, pointed nose, this threatened reptile is extremely distinctive. Much of its habitat has been lost to shoreline development, so Ontario's softshells are left to depend on sites like the Thames to survive.

There are many spots from which hikers can access the trail along its length. Start at London's Ivey Park, follow the river northward to Harris Park, and then cross the river at Blackfriars Street. Wander the opposite bank back south to Riverside Park. Kensington Bridge returns you to your starting point.

Wheatley Provincial Park

A Carolinian adventure in Ontario's 'deep south' provincial park

What Makes This Hot Spot Hot?

- It's a prime example of Carolinian forest and home to several species of southern tree.
- Wheatley is close to the epicentre of southern Ontario's spring bird migration.
- After dark, listen to calling eastern screech-owls from your campsite.

Address: 21116 Klondyke Road, P.O. Box 640, Wheatley, ON N0P 2P0
Tel.: (519) 825-4659
Website: ontarioparks.com/park/wheatley

Open mid-April to mid-October

↗ **Guess who's visiting your campsite? It's an eastern screech-owl.**

Sharing the same latitude as northern California, Wheatley Provincial Park is located in the Carolinian Forest Region, a Canadian forest type that occurs only in southern Ontario. This "deep south" park is an ideal place to learn more about a handful of southern trees that make their home here yet are far more common in the United States. One of these is the black gum, also known as the black tupelo. With its deeply furrowed bark, alternate leaves and beautiful red to purplish fall colour, the black gum also harbours a secret: This species can be incredibly long-lived. A New Hampshire specimen was found to be 679 years old, making the black gum eastern North America's oldest flowering tree.

Another Carolinian tree found at Wheatley is the sassafras. The sassafras is one of the most identifiable trees in Ontario, thanks to its specially shaped leaves, which are unlike those of any other tree found in the province. Some are simple with no lobes; others have two (these leaves resemble a mitten) or three lobes. The distinctive tulip tree—the only tree in Ontario with pointed four-lobed leaves—is also found here.

The 241-hectare park features two kilometres of

observe water birds, aquatic mammals and fish. In the spring, Wheatley is a popular camping destination because so many birds pass through this area during migration. But don't ignore the appeal of Wheatley's resident birds. Just after dark, listen carefully and you may hear the eastern screech-owls calling. These small owls have two main call patterns. A long, fluid, wavering trill called the tremolo is a contact call that mated pairs use to keep track of each other in the darkness. The other call is a descending whinny that is used as a territorial signal to keep other screech-owls out of the pairs' territory.

sandy beach and a network of creeks; hiking trails and footbridges allow visitors to explore wetlands to better

↑ **The sumac's brilliant red colour dresses up the October shoreline at Wheatley.**

← **An autumn sassafras leaf.**

Central Ontario South

Cawthra Mulock Nature Reserve

Thanks to forward-thinking private citizens, a wildlife haven thrives in the midst of human activities

What Makes This Hot Spot Hot?

- It's a wildlife haven in an agricultural and urban landscape.
- Explore different habitats that support different wildlife species.
- Cawthra Mulock is a great example of the importance of land donations to Ontario Nature.

Address: North of Oak Ridges Moraine. Access west entrance at 18580 Dufferin Street or east entrance at 18462 Bathurst Street
Tel.: (416) 444-8419
Website: ontarionature. org/protect/habitat/ cawthra_mulock.php

Open year-round

↗ **A metallic green sweat bee enjoys a taste of goldenrod nectar.**

Donated to Ontario Nature in 2003, the Cawthra Mulock Nature Reserve is a perfect example of how private land-owners can make a difference to area wildlife. Located just north of Newmarket, these 108 hectares are surrounded by urban development as well as agricultural fields, which makes the reserve's forests and meadows an invaluable haven for animals. There are wetland areas here, too, including a pond and two creeks that are a part of the West Holland River watershed.

A network of trails leads visitors through a range of habitats. A spring walk reveals spring ephemeral wildflowers such as white trilliums, jack-in-the-pulpit, wild ginger and bloodroot under the canopy of the mature maple-beech forest. The open fields and stream and pond edges are promising places to look for spring and summer invertebrates. Check

the plants along the streams for the longjawed orbweaver spider or ebony jewelwing damselfly. You might also find a cecropia moth, Canada's largest moth species, hanging in the hawthorn trees nearby. Bird lovers should watch for field specialists such as the bobolink and eastern meadowlark, both threatened species in Ontario.

In the fall, the fields are full of blooming goldenrod and asters. These attract pollinating insects such as honey bees, bumble bees, hover flies, butterflies and beetles. They, in turn, attract many small predators such as crab spiders, praying mantids, assassin bugs and stink bugs. During a winter hike, look for the tracks of the coyote, red fox, white-tailed deer and snowshoe hare. Throughout the year, Cawthra Mulock provides secure habitat for wildlife, all thanks to the generosity and vision of the previous landowners.

↑ **Check out the streams here for plants and invertebrates.**

Crawford Lake Conservation Area

A place where naturalists have explored for centuries

What Makes This Hot Spot Hot?

- Visitors can learn about a meromictic lake.
- Explore a restored Iroquoian village with longhouses and other cultural artifacts.
- The site features a number of trails from which you can look for wildflowers and wildlife.

Address: 3115 Conservation Road, Milton, ON L9T 2X3
Tel.: (905) 854-0234
Website: conservationhalton.ca/crawford-lake

Open year-round

→ **The deep, peaceful waters of Crawford Lake, a meromictic lake in Halton Region.**

Crawford Lake itself harboured the clue that eventually led to an indigenous village's discovery. Known as a "meromictic lake," Crawford is so deep and has such a small surface area that wind action fails to stir up the water at its lowest levels or to introduce oxygen to the lake's depths. As a result, much of the sediment and other debris that has sunk to the bottom over time has been perfectly preserved in layers. In their efforts to accurately age these layers, scientists discovered corn pollen, and so began the search for signs of an ancient village whose inhabitants were farmers.

Today, visitors to the Crawford Lake Conservation Area have a chance to walk in the footsteps of people who were a part of this landscape long before Europeans arrived in North America. Once home to a community of Iroquoian people, the village originally featured 11 longhouses; three of these have been painstakingly reconstructed on their original footprint and feature historically accurate cultural artifacts. As you explore the site, remember that the tree species you see, the birds you hear and the forest smells you inhale are the same ones these residents lived among 500 years ago.

The conservation area has many trails for wandering, but be sure to take the 1.4-kilometre Crawford Lake Trail down to the lake during your visit. Here, a raised boardwalk protects the shoreline but allows you to get a great look at the whole lake. As you walk along, pause at any spot along the shore and take a moment to imagine, half a millennium ago, someone else enjoying and appreciating the same view.

Forks of the Credit Provincial Park

On the Bruce Trail and easily accessible from the GTA, this little-known park is a hidden gem with lots to offer

What Makes This Hot Spot Hot?

- The park features an unusual collection of different habitats, hosting a diversity of uncommon wildlife.
- The scenery is memorable, especially the waterfall overlook.
- It's a lightly used park with lots of room to roam and no crowds.

Address: Caledon, ON L7K 2H8
Tel.: (705) 435-2498
Website: ontarioparks.com/park/forksofthecredit

Open year-round

↗ **The well-named violet dancer alights.**

As its name suggests, Forks of the Credit Provincial Park follows the beautiful Credit River as it winds through a gorge and over a spectacular waterfall. The lands surrounding the river are a mosaic of unusual habitats, including glacial features such as a kettle lake and kame hills. Here, rolling pastures are gradually being reclaimed by encroaching forest.

The natural features of the park attract equally eclectic wildlife populations. Rare grassland birds call the pastures home, including the secretive clay-coloured sparrow and the threatened bobolink. An array of showy wildflowers grows in the pastures, attracting butterflies of every size and shade. The kettle lake almost overflows with frogs, and one can regularly spot a garter or water snake plunging beneath its surface.

The Credit River itself is home to a fantastic diversity

of dragonflies and damselflies, including riverine specialities like the robust spiketails and delicate dancers. Beneath the ripples and eddies, brown and brook trout feed and spawn, and fly fishermen can sometimes be seen trying their luck. The forests at the river's edge are a stopover for migrant birds, and kingfishers regularly patrol the banks in search of their next meal.

Forks of the Credit is a day-use-only provincial park, having no campsites. The park is not regularly staffed, and facilities are limited to privy washrooms and a few picnic tables. A voluntary pay system exists at the park entrance and trailhead off McLaren Road. While this lack of amenities may be off-putting to some, don't let it turn you away from this stunning park. A day spent at Forks of the Credit will put a smile on your face and have you coming back for more before you know it.

↑ **A brown trout hovers over riverbed vegetation in the Credit River.**

Happy Valley Forest

A reservoir of biodiversity in the GTA

What Makes This Hot Spot Hot?

- Happy Valley Forest represents one of the region's best opportunities for establishing a mature forest.
- The forest contains a wide variety of habitats and species.
- An enormous carbon sink, this forest sucks up carbon dioxide emissions from commuters travelling on Hwy 400.

Address: North of Vaughn on Hwy 400. For directions to Happy Valley Forest, visit: natureconservancy.ca/assets/documents/on/HVFMap.pdf
Tel.: N/A
Website: natureconservancy.ca/en/where-we-work/ontario/our-work/happy_valley_forest.html

Open year-round

↗ **A wooded swamp and wetland in Happy Valley.**

One of the largest remaining intact hardwood forests on the Oak Ridges Moraine—a massive ridge that stretches from the Niagara Escarpment to the Trent River—Happy Valley Forest is a boldly textured landscape. North of Vaughn on Hwy 400, this steeply rolling terrain features an upland forest, old fields, a handful of creek valleys, wooded swamps and wetlands, all distributed over an impressive 1,150 hectares.

In combination, its size and diversity mean that the forest has the capacity to withstand and rebound from natural disturbances such as wildfires, severe weather and disease. In 50 years, Happy Valley may well be a healthy example of a mature forest—a natural reservoir for biodiversity.

The Nature Conservancy of Canada (NCC) has spent decades protecting large sections of the Oak Ridges Moraine, and more than 100 hectares of that land are in

Happy Valley Forest. NCC's intention is to create and manage an even larger heritage forest that will become a model for mature-forest ecology and stewardship. Today, walkers and hikers along the forest trails can enjoy the many early benefits of that strategy.

In spring, the forest floor is festooned with trilliums. Overhead, the birdsong of more than 110 breeding species, including nationally significant birds such as the Acadian fly-catcher and cerulean warbler and the threatened hooded warbler and red-shouldered hawk, may be heard. Rustling underfoot in the damp leaf litter, a red eft, the terrestrial stage of the aquatic adult red-spotted newt, might show itself. As you emerge from the dappled light of the mixed forest, you can wander through a meadow where butterflies flit in the sun. And in the lowland wetlands, take note of the small kettle ponds and depressions, remnants of glacial melt-waters from the last ice age.

↑ Briefly on land in its early life, the red eft eventually ends up as the aquatic red-spotted newt.

↖ In spring, white trilliums carpet the forest floor.

Humber Arboretum and the West Humber River Valley

An elegant blend of natural and cultivated beauty

What Makes This Hot Spot Hot?

- Public transportation drops off visitors at the Humber Arboretum entrance.
- The arboretum gardens and natural areas exist side by side.
- White-tailed deer are often seen on the trails.

Address: 205 Humber College Blvd., Toronto, ON M9W 5L7
Tel.: (416) 675-5009
Website: humberarboretum. on.ca

Open year-round

A collaborative project between the Humber Arboretum, the City of Toronto and the Toronto and Region Conservation Authority, this area merges the managed beauty of ornamental gardens with wilder trails that explore forests and the West Humber River.

Launched by Humber College horticulture students in 1977, the Humber Arboretum is utilized for education as well as research projects. Just as importantly, it is open to the public and is a popular spot for walks and hikes. At just over 100 hectares, it is filled with botanical collections that feature woody and herbaceous plants of both native and non-native origins. Six kilometres of trails wind through gardens and forests and over bridges and stone pathways, making it a wonderful place to visit in all four seasons. In spring, the garden flowers and showy woody plants burst into bloom, while in summer, the ponds are busy with aquatic life. By fall, the autumn leaves crunch beneath your feet. In winter, you might cross paths with a white-tailed deer.

A paved trail along the river leads all the way to Lake Ontario, 20 kilometres away. En route, the trail and bridges offer exceptional opportunities for watching river wildlife such as beavers, herons, waterfowl, turtles and frogs. The trail passes through a significant deciduous forest of hickory, maple, ash and beech trees that provides cover for spring and fall migrating songbirds and ephemeral spring wildflowers. During the winter, keep your eyes peeled here and in the conifers near the arboretum for the long-eared owl. This medium-sized owl species likes to hunt in open areas but seeks out dense

roosting sites during the day to hide from mobbing jays and crows. The long-eared owl looks very much like the more common great horned owl but for the vertical streaks on its breasts and—you guessed it—its longer ear tufts.

↑ During the day, a long-eared owl hides in plain sight.

Luther Marsh Wildlife Management Area

An important inland wetland complex that attracts an abundance of wildlife

What Makes This Hot Spot Hot?

- The reservoir encompasses many habitats with lots of areas for visitors to explore.
- For those who enjoy tracking, a winter visit provides lots of different mammal species to identify and follow.
- Sandhill cranes are commonly seen here and are a perfect subject for the wildlife photographer.

Address: 034588 Sideroad 21-22 Grand Valley, ON L9W 0H2
Tel.: (519) 928-2832
Website: grandriver.ca/index/document.cfm?Sec=27&Sub1=128&Sub2=0

Open year-round

↗ **A meadow jumping mouse pauses just long enough to be photographed before bounding out of sight.**

While most of southern Ontario's significant wetlands are found along a Great Lake shoreline, this great reservoir is an exception. Situated at the headwaters of the Grand River watershed, Luther Marsh is a 5,200-hectare area that includes marshes, swamps, fields and forests. These extensive habitats are home to common and rare species—anything could turn up. Visitors might see porcupines, snowshoe hares, muskrats, beavers, white-tailed deer and mink among Luther's mammal populations. If you're lucky, you might catch a glimpse of an uncommon small mammal, perhaps a northern flying squirrel or a meadow jumping mouse. In a snowy winter, there are exceptional tracking opportunities, with many species to identify and follow.

During the summer months, Luther is a dragonfly lover's dream. Many species live here, and at certain times of the year, the skies are cloudy

with species with names such as baskettail, white-face, clubtail and darner. For those with a lepidopteran bent, there are many butterflies and moths as well.

The great blue heron is the mainstay of any marsh, and Luther is also home to a large heronry. This is an ideal place to watch these magnificent birds in numbers. But keep your distance from the heronry itself—young herons might topple from their nests if frightened. Watching an adult hunt for food, however, is the perfect way to get to know these birds. Showing remarkable patience, an adult waits for a fish or frog to come just close enough before spearing it with its formidable beak. Once it has had its fill, the heron flies back to the nest and regurgitates a meal to its hungry young.

Scan the area carefully, and you might also see one or two of the white great egrets that now call Luther home.

↑ Resident deer take a drink at the edge of the marsh.

Rattray Marsh Conservation Area

At Lake Ontario's west end, this urban marsh purifies and replenishes the groundwater and nurtures a remarkable number of species

What Makes This Hot Spot Hot?

- Surrounded on three sides by the activities of modern city life, it is a peaceful marshland respite.
- This protected marsh filters and purifies water—naturally.
- Rattray Marsh provides habitat for hundreds of species of flora and fauna.

Address: 50 Bexhill Road, Mississauga, ON L5H 3L1
Tel.: (800) 367-0890
Website: creditvalleyca.ca

Open year-round (after sunrise and before sunset)

Rattray Marsh is one of the last remaining baymouth bar coastal wetlands at the western end of Lake Ontario. Defended against developers more than 50 years ago, the marsh has been a popular destination for generations of nature-loving Mississauga residents. It is owned and operated by Credit Valley Conservation, but the voluntary work of the Rattray Marsh Protection Association is a critical piece in the ongoing protection and preservation of this unusual lakeside treasure.

Spanning roughly 38 hectares of lakeshore, field and woodland habitat, the conservation area has 3.3 kilometres of trail and boardwalk, including a section of waterfront trail that allows visitors to explore the property without damaging sensitive habitat. A wildflower meadow bursts with colour in spring, and strollers can pause at a lookout point and gaze at the marsh as it enters Lake Ontario. A refuge for aquatic life and migrating waterfowl, the marsh is alive with birdlife, with sightings of the red-throated loon, pied-billed grebe, great egret, canvasback, killdeer and spotted

sandpiper, among many others. The marsh also provides critical spawning habitat for pike and other species.

Visitors can access a short boardwalk loop that provides a second popular vantage point for marsh life and spring ephemeral flowers. Yet another trail winds through a mature forest community of

sugar maple, beech and oak and then past the Sheridan Creek floodplain and swamp.

On the shore of one of southern Ontario's largest cities, Rattray Marsh serves as a peaceful and restorative introduction to one of our most essential ecosystems.

←↑ **Open four seasons of the year, the Rattray Marsh is built for visitors.**

Rouge National Urban Park

For city dwellers, the natural wonderland of a lifetime

What Makes This Hot Spot Hot?

- This huge park is within driving distance of one-fifth of Canada's population.
- The Rouge is home to an abundance of species, both familiar and uncommon.
- It is the first national park to be established in an urban area.

For directions to Rouge Park, visit rougepark.com/explore/plan/directions.php
Tel.: (905) 713-6038
Website: parkscanada.ca/rouge

Open year-round

↗ Autumn colour in Canada's first national urban park.

In a collection that celebrates Ontario's nature hot spots, it would be impossible to ignore the Rouge. In reality, there are countless hot spots in this vast urban park, which is currently a sprawling 40 square kilometres that stretches from the Oak Ridges Moraine to Lake Ontario, with the Rouge River system as its centrepiece.

Situated near 20 percent of Canada's population, the Rouge National Urban Park is explicitly regarded as an opportunity for city-dwelling Canadians to connect with the country's natural heritage. The Rouge has been protected by decades of dedicated local stewardship, but with federal involvement come collaborative aquatic habitat enhancement, wetland restoration, native plantings and the protection of threatened species, among other initiatives.

The Rouge is a crazy quilt of landscapes, from rivers and creeks, geological outcrops, hoodoos and gullies, drumlins and flutes to high-level terraces, marshes, woodlands and meadows, right down to the sandy spit where the Rouge River flows into Lake Ontario. The sheer habitat variety of the park leads naturally to biodiversity. Rouge Park has that in abundance, with more than 750 plant species and over 325

↑ A wetland vista in the Rouge.

species of birds, fish, mammals, reptiles and amphibians, many of which are nationally and regionally rare.

Via a network of trails, visitors can hike through old-growth forest and woodlands as red squirrels race up and down the trees, can listen to a bobolink or a yellow warbler in a quiet, leafy glen and can view a red-tailed hawk surveying the landscape from on high. In the early morning and early evening, the sounds of spring peepers and grey tree frogs fill the air, and in spring and summer, the buzzing of insects reverberates all around. Lookouts offer panoramic views of the bluffs and river valleys. For residents of the Greater Toronto Area, it's a backyard wonderland that could take a lifetime to explore.

↑ Canada geese take flight in the fall.

Scarborough Bluffs

Human activity has put this significant geological feature under siege

What Makes This Hot Spot Hot?

- The Scarborough Bluffs have been described as a geological record of the last ice age.
- On the Doris McCarthy Trail, hikers can investigate the Bellamy Ravine from top to bottom.
- The Waterfront Trail offers impressive views of the bluffs from below.

Address: Scarborough, ON
Tel.: (416) 338-5058
Website: ontariotrails. on.ca/trails/view/ scarborough-bluffs-trail

Open year-round

Elizabeth Simcoe, the wife of Upper Canada's first lieutenant governor, described the dramatic escarpment on Lake Ontario as "extremely bold." It's still an apt description for the Scarborough Bluffs today, especially when this impressive feature is seen from the lake.

Rising some 100 metres along 15 kilometres of lakeshore, the Scarborough Bluffs emerged from sediments amassed during the last stages of the most recent ice age. At their base, the bluffs hold ancient plant and animal fossils deposited in a river delta during the first advance of the Wisconsin Glaciation. On top of these are alternating layers of boulder clay and sand, which scientists say represent four advances and retreats of the ice sheet.

Ravines, trails, meadowland, woodland and beaches characterize the area. There are a number of bluff-top parks, and one of the few points of access to the shoreline from the northern end is the Doris

McCarthy Trail, which allows visitors to explore the Bellamy Ravine. Home to regionally rare plant species, such as downy ryegrass and russet buffaloberry, the ravine also

provides habitat for deer, foxes and coyotes and resident and migratory populations of birds. Farther south is the massive convex cliff of clay and sand known as Cathedral Bluffs, deeply cut with gullies that have left the spires for which it is named. At the sandy beach at Bluffer's Park, the bluffs serve as a dramatic backdrop.

The City of Scarborough grew up around the bluffs, and as the cliffs have eroded year by year, lakeview properties have been increasingly compromised.

As with most fragile habitats, efforts to protect the bluffs have not always had the desired outcome. Stabilizing strategies along the beach to thwart the eroding action of the waves have interrupted the natural cycle; landfill has plugged former ravines, and even as vegetation stabilizes the cliff slope, it obscures the geological features that make the bluffs remarkable. The challenge has been set: Will the bluffs be regarded as "extremely bold" long into the future?

←↑ Two "extremely bold" views of the geological wonder that is the Scarborough Bluffs.

Seaton Trail

On the outskirts of Pickering, this trail features bracing sections of true wilderness

What Makes This Hot Spot Hot?

- It's a slice of wilderness near a densely populated section of the GTA.
- The trail provides occasional steep challenges to hikers and bikers.
- From birds and beavers to fish and turtles, animals are active all along the trail.

Address: West Duffins Creek, Pickering
Tel.: N/A
Website: seatontrail.org

Open year-round

↗ **A barred owl stakes out its territory in a trailside tree.**

For residents seeking refuge from the ever-expanding Greater Toronto Area, the 13-kilometre Seaton Trail has long been a valued natural outlet. Built in the 1970s by high school and university students working with what is now the Toronto Region Conservation Authority (TRCA), the trail follows the West Duffins Creek valley northwest of Pickering. Once maintained by Boy Scouts attending an area camp, it is now largely overseen by the volunteer efforts of the Friends of Seaton Trail in cooperation with the TRCA and a collection of stakeholders eager to monitor, maintain and improve the trail and watershed.

The trail echoes the historic hunting and fishing routes along the creek established by generations of indigenous people, from the earliest nomadic Paleo-Indian residents to Archaic peoples, Algonquian-speaking tribes and the Lake Ontario Iroquois.

Today, a common entry point is from Whitevale Park. Heading north on the trail is an easy hike to the dam, while a more challenging route is to follow the creek. Past the dam, the trail leads to the parking lot at Green River.

South of Whitevale, the terrain quickly grows tougher. With rough, unstable surfaces,

the rugged route features steep bluffs and eroded embankments punctuated with dramatic views. The creek is home to rainbow trout in the spring, brook trout in summer and Chinook salmon and brown trout in the fall. Along the shore, you might spot a painted turtle sunning itself. As you approach the final section of the trail to Grand Valley Park, the walking is easy, and you'll have a chance to appreciate a variety of habitats.

The Seaton Trail is a favourite spot for hikers and dog walkers, but the impressive vantage points, fields of wildflowers and active wildlife attract nature lovers as well.

↑ Wild and rugged in places, peaceful in others, this trail is full of engaging challenges for hikers.

Terra Cotta Conservation Area

Brick-red stream bottoms, tranquil trails and peaceful ponds

What Makes This Hot Spot Hot?

- There is a variety of trails for all skill levels.
- Visitors can explore a number of wetland areas.
- During the winter months, travel the trails on rented cross-country skis or snowshoes.

Address: 14452 Winston Churchill Blvd., Halton Hills, ON LoP 1No
Tel.: (905) 877-1120
Website: creditvalleyca. ca/enjoy-the-outdoors/ conservation-areas/terra-cotta-conservation-area

Open year-round, conditions permitting

↗ **Don't let the smile fool you: This American bullfrog is a powerful predator.**

→ **An easy-going trail wraps around Wolf Lake.**

Terra Cotta Conservation Area is yet another Niagara Escarpment hot spot that seems to have been created for the naturalist's enjoyment. This 196-hectare site has 12 kilometres of trails that range in difficulty from easy to hard. For instance, the Terra Cotta Lane trail that winds around Wolf Lake is quite flat and navigable, while the A.F. Coventry trail features a series of elevation changes and requires a bit more effort. While hiking here, you may see how Terra Cotta got its name: The streambeds are lined with brick-red shale the rich colour of terra cotta pots.

While you won't hear wolves at Wolf Lake (the lake was actually named after a former area manager), listen for another northern songster resident here: the American bullfrog. This huge amphibian is one of North America's largest frogs, and its deep resonating "jug-a-rum" song is a particular favourite among naturalists. It surprises many to find out that bullfrogs are major predators that dine on everything from dragonflies and damselflies to other frogs, small snakes and even small rodents. While you're visiting Terra Cotta, take time to sit and watch one of these behemoths—you may see one leap into predatory action.

Take the opportunity to get to know a little more about the local trees. There are some excellent specimens of shagbark hickory along the trails—watch out for their very shaggy bark peeling from the trunks in long strips. Red oaks are also found at Terra Cotta, and in the fall you're sure to see acorns strewn about on the forest floor—if the squirrels haven't gotten to them first.

Thickson's Woods Nature Reserve

Home to the last old-growth white pines on Lake Ontario's northern shore, this small woodlot is a sanctuary for migrating birds

What Makes This Hot Spot Hot?

- Its towering white pines are the last surviving old-growth pines on the northern shore of Lake Ontario.
- A stopover for many species of migrating birds, the woodlot is also home to diverse plant and animal communities.
- A visit to Thickson's Woods offers an easy and accessible walk through a wide variety of habitats.

Address: Waterfront Trail, Whitby, ON L1N 9Z7
Tel.: N/A
Website: thicksonswoods.com

Open year-round

The towering white pines at Thickson's Woods were once officially reserved as ship masts for the Royal Navy, but before the trees were collected, sail-powered naval ships disappeared. With no market for their broad trunks, the white pines stood unbothered for decades, looming over the understorey and providing habitat for wildlife. But in 1983, as developers encroached on the area, the logging rights were sold: It appeared that Thickson's Woods would stand no more.

In an impressive feat, a small group of concerned naturalists raised the money to buy the property. Although some of the pines had already been felled, others remain today, 150 years in age and exceeding 30 metres in height. These giants define the woodlot, and the gaps left by their fallen brethren have been filled by other tree species, including black cherry, blue beech and

mountain maple. In 2001, the naturalists—now working on behalf of the Thickson's Woods Land Trust—purchased the meadow adjacent to the woodlot, creating the nature reserve we see today.

While the reserve is rich in all varieties of life, it is especially important as a rest stop and fuelling station for migrating birds. The tall pines may act as a landmark, drawing tired migrants in with the promise of refuge. In the spring and fall, the trees come alive with warblers, vireos, flycatchers and thrushes, while raptors and waterfowl move overhead. Not all birdlife at Thickson's Woods is temporary, though. Many birds breed here, including forest specialists like the wood thrush and red-eyed vireo. Visitors with keen eyes may even spot resident great horned owls, blending in among the foliage.

Thickson's Woods is open every day and free of charge. The trails are well established, and the walking is easy. The reserve is not staffed, so be prepared to explore this small woodlot on your own. For those seeking an introduction to the woods, the Land Trust hosts a nature festival each September.

←↑ All creatures great and small: In Thickson's Woods, the diminutive black-throated blue warbler and the great horned owl both make a good living.

Tommy Thompson Park

An accidental wilderness in the heart of the Ontario's largest city

What Makes This Hot Spot Hot?

- Just minutes from downtown, Tommy Thompson Park is one of the largest natural areas on the Toronto waterfront.
- A hot spot for migrating and breeding birds, the park hosts some of the best birdwatching in the GTA.
- A bird banding station and annual nature festivals provide great opportunities to experience the park's wildlife.

Address: 1 Leslie Street, Toronto, ON   M4M 3M2
Tel.: (416) 661-6600
Website: tommythompsonpark.ca

Open year-round

It is difficult to imagine humbler beginnings than those of Tommy Thompson Park. The Leslie Street Spit upon which it sits was not built as a nature sanctuary but as a breakwater for Toronto's Outer Harbour. It was constructed with dredged material from the harbour itself and rubble from construction projects within the city. Over time, nature began to invade the barren landscape, and advocacy groups arose to secure the spit's status as an urban wilderness.

There is little on the Leslie Street Spit to remind the visitor of its origins, save for the concrete debris that makes up its cobble beaches. The surface of the spit is blanketed in cottonwood forests, wildflower meadows and wetlands, and it plays host to a spectacular diversity of wildlife. Birds are perhaps the greatest draw, with more than 300 species having been identified on the site. The spit is a vital migration stopover for songbirds and boasts breeding habitat for uncommon water birds

like the American wood-cock, sora, Virginia rail and black-crowned night-heron.

Tommy Thompson Park covers the northern half of the spit and is open to visitors on weekends year-round, free of charge. Vehicles are not permitted in the park, making it a haven for pedestrians and cyclists. There are over 23 kilometres of trails, including many that are accessible to strollers and wheelchairs. The Toronto and Region Conservation Authority operates a bird banding station that is open to visitors and organizes annual bird and butterfly festivals to introduce the uninitiated to the park's wildlife-viewing opportunities.

←↑ Black-crowned night-herons roost in the canopy at this unusual wildlife park, where the city skyline is never far from sight.

Toronto Botanical Garden

Connect with plants and learn how to create a garden oasis in your own yard at this urban refuge

What Makes This Hot Spot Hot?

- In the heart of Canada's largest city, it's a place to learn to grow plants.
- There's practical advice on how to choose natural examples for your own yard.
- It's a peaceful refuge from the city's crowded streets and sidewalks.

Address: 777 Lawrence Avenue East, Toronto, ON M3C 1P2
Tel.: (416) 397-1340
Website: torontobotanicalgarden.ca

Open year-round (check holiday schedule on website)

🚶 🔭

↗ **A hint of Alice in Wonderland: a sundial in the shape of a monarch butterfly.**

The Toronto Botanical Gardens "exists to encourage, inspire and inform gardeners." And it certainly does that. Located right in the City of Toronto, these gardens were opened to the public in 1956 and have been a mecca for urban gardeners ever since. The programs and displays offer property owners guidance on how to transform a private yard into a garden oasis. The value of a restorative green space, especially within the city limits of a huge city, can readily be seen during a wander through the gardens here.

The Teaching Garden is made up of many small gardens and is used to help children understand plants. It's a perfect place to get the kid in your life connected to the green world. The Spiral Butterfly Garden not only shows how the sun is important for plant growth but features plants that attract butterflies as well. The Dinosaur Garden has species that

the Earth's early inhabitants might have found tasty, while the Sensory Garden adds a real hands-on (and nose-on) dimension to your visit.

Naturalists should make sure to drop in on Nature's Garden, which re-creates two different southern Ontario habitats: the Carolinian Forest and the Great Lakes-St. Lawrence Forest. By changing the soil chemistry to either alkaline or acidic, staff gardeners have been able to plant native Ontario species such as sassafras, bush honeysuckle and blueberries. These plants, in turn, attract wildlife for food and/or shelter, which many cityscapes lack. Another spot to check out is the Woodland Walk and Bird Habitat, where visitors are invited to enjoy the shelter of the trees and escape the hectic urban landscape on the corner of Lawrence and Leslie. Along the trail, you'll encounter many native plants among the ornamental ones.

↑ At the Toronto Botanical Garden, Nature's Garden showcases two distinct habitats that form part of Toronto's native plant heritage—the Carolinian Forest and the Great Lakes-St. Lawrence Forest.

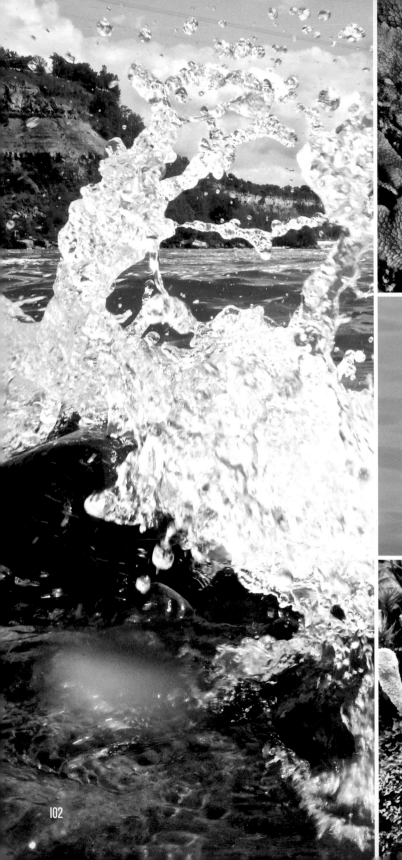

Niagara Region

1. Ball's Falls Conservation Area
2. Beamer Memorial Conservation Area
3. Niagara Glen Nature Reserve
4. Niagara River
5. Short Hills Provincial Park
6. Wainfleet Bog Conservation Area
7. Woodend Conservation Area

Ball's Falls Conservation Area

On the Niagara Escarpment, two dramatic cataracts with very different personalities

What Makes This Hot Spot Hot?

- The lower cataract is two-thirds the size of Niagara Falls.
- A hike upstream takes visitors to the smaller, undisturbed upper falls.
- Visitors can tour a reconstructed pioneer village with an operating flour mill, blacksmith shop, lime kiln and family home.

Address: 3292 Sixth Avenue, Lincoln, ON LoR 1So
Tel.: (905) 562-5235
Website: infoniagara.com/recreation/balls_falls/balls_falls.aspx

Open year-round

Named for brothers John and George Ball, who settled here in the late 1780s and eventually built a large gristmill at the lower waterfall, the hamlet that grew up around Ball's Falls in the early 19th century has been lovingly restored and is promoted as the perfect site for a storybook wedding. But nature lovers agree that the true attraction of the 80-hectare Ball's Falls Conservation Area rests with its spectacular setting on the Niagara Escarpment, which comes with its own rich natural legacy.

The centrepiece of the conservation area is not one but two impressive cataracts. The main event is the lower falls, which dramatically plunges some 25 metres over the Niagara Escarpment into a pool on Twenty Mile Creek. The hardy limestone foundation directly underlying the waterfall defends the fragile rock layers beneath it against the surging creek and the sediments and stones it

sweeps along in its path. The layered walls surrounding the waterfall and pool are a composite of limestone, dolostone, shale and sandstone, each a distinct colour.

Frequent visitors to Ball's Falls also enthusiastically promote the more modest 11-metre-high upper falls. Described as undisturbed, its wild, untended setting adds to its appeal, and the one-kilometre hike upstream

to see it allows visitors to get a good look at the many small potholes that dot the riverbed en route. Keep in mind that the flow of water over each waterfall is seasonal: The creek's torrential flow in early spring can retreat to a mere trickle in the drier summer months.

Also highly recommended is the Cataract Trail, which forms a loop from the west side of the bridge across Twenty Mile Creek to the upper falls

and back. One section runs along the creek; the other takes visitors inland, where they can enjoy the mixed forest. Songbirds sing among coniferous trees and butternut, black walnut, shagbark hickory and occasional rare species such as sycamore and pignut hickory. A wide variety of plants can be found along the trail, from green and white trilliums to Virginia bluebells, wild leek and wild columbine.

←↑ There are two lovely waterfalls to enjoy at Ball's Falls: the towering lower falls and the more understated but wildly beautiful upper falls.

Beamer Memorial Conservation Area

Get a bird's eye view of migrating raptors while exploring the Niagara Escarpment

What Makes This Hot Spot Hot?

- Welcome spring by watching raptors as they wing their way back to their northern nesting sites.
- Visit on Good Friday and be a part of the Niagara Peninsula Hawkwatch Open House.
- Hike a section of the Niagara Escarpment's Bruce Trail.

Address: Quarry Road, Grimsby, ON L3M 4E7
Tel.: (905) 788-3135
Websites: npca.ca/conservation-areas/beamer-memorial, niagarapeninsulahawkwatch.org

Open year-round

↗ **In flight, a northern harrier shows off the white patch at the base of its tail.**

Most hawk-watching sites in Ontario are popular in the fall, but Beamer Memorial Conservation Area is famously a spring raptor observation site. When northward flying hawks, eagles, vultures, harriers, falcons and osprey reach the south shore of Lake Erie or Lake Ontario, they are unable to use warm rising air currents (known as thermals) to cross the open water. Instead, they fly along the coast and are eventually funnelled through the Niagara peninsula, where the Niagara Escarpment provides lift for the birds through wind deflected upward off its cliffs.

This is the place to learn how to identify raptors flying overhead. From March 1 to mid-May, knowledgeable naturalists from Niagara Peninsula Hawkwatch are stationed at a special observation platform, eager to teach you the ways in which shape, flight pattern and markings are all useful clues to sleuthing out a definitive raptor I.D. Watch for the thick dark and thin light bands on the tail of a red-shouldered hawk, the white rump of a northern harrier or the upheld, two-toned wings of a turkey vulture.

A hike along the trails at Beamer leads to overlook platforms right on the escarpment edge. From here, you may

have a chance to look down on some of the hawks from above, a very different vantage point. You can also enjoy an impressive panorama of the Lake Ontario shoreline, and a springtime hike might reveal your first-of-the-year eastern garter snake or mourning cloak butterfly. The conservation area also features Forty Mile Creek's Upper and Lower Beamer Falls as well as an opportunity to hike a section of the famous Bruce Trail.

↑ At Beamer, visitors can enjoy the trail and Forty Mile Creek's Upper and Lower Beamer Falls.

Niagara Glen Nature Reserve

An international border, a raging river and a biological hot spot

What Makes This Hot Spot Hot?

- It's home to many species of at-risk flora and fauna.
- Visitors can get close to a valuable river ecosystem with Class 5 and 6 rapids.
- Ontario's only population of the northern dusky salamander depends on the Gorge's cold-water seeps for survival.

Address: 3050 Niagara River Parkway, Niagara Falls, ON L2E 6S4
Tel.: (905) 354-6678
Website: niagaraparks. com/niagara-falls-attractions/niagara-parks-nature-centre.html

Open year-round

↗ **Plants underfoot at the Niagara Glen Nature Reserve include the liverwort, a flowerless, spore-producing simple plant.**

It's impossible to stand on the Canadian side of the 11-kilometre-long Niagara Gorge without appreciating the dramatic view of the United States across the turquoise water that churns below. But don't be so distracted by the scene's grandeur that you miss out on the fascinating world at your feet. About a minute's walk past the nature centre pavilion, enter the Niagara Glen Nature Reserve via a winding metal staircase down the cliff face. At the bottom, a network of marked trails leads through Carolinian forest and down to the raging river that has been carving its way back to Niagara Falls for the past 12,500 years.

Proceed with care—a stunning variety of invaluable habitats nestle on the slopes of the deep Niagara Gorge. Diverse and sometimes other-worldly-looking communities of bryophytes (non-vascular plants that reproduce via spores rather than flowers or seeds) can be seen crowding the cold-water

seeps and trickles. These saturated pockets between the rocks and old-growth trees provide habitat for the endangered northern dusky salamander, an amphibian that doesn't occur anywhere else in Ontario. The Gorge's complex ecosystem supports a myriad of flora and fauna that appeal to the keen naturalist and curious visitor alike. Bald eagles, beavers and milk snakes can all be seen here.

In early spring, watch as vehicle-sized icebergs shoot the Class 5 and 6 rapids en route to Lake Ontario. As spring becomes summer, wildlife spotting is easy, though once the leaves mature in summer, visitors may feel they're enveloped in a giant green cloak. Up above, a chance opening in the canopy could reveal turkey vultures soaring on thermal updrafts. In fall, tulip trees and other deciduous species silently explode into dazzling colours. When snow settles in, the trails become more challenging but are still remarkably rewarding to the seasoned winter hiker.

↑ **It's hard to look away from the surging waters of the Niagara River.**

Niagara River

Gulling along the Gorge

What Makes This Hot Spot Hot?

- There's a greater variety of gulls at Niagara during this season than anywhere else on Earth.
- There are amazing views of the Gorge walls, the rushing river and the three waterfalls that make up Niagara Falls.
- Once your birding day is done, visit any one of the region's excellent wineries and restaurants.

Address: Niagara-on-the-Lake, south shore of Lake Ontario, at the mouth of the Niagara River

Open year-round

↗ **An immature black-legged kittiwake drops in on Niagara.**

Even the most resistant naturalist eventually falls under the spell of gull identification, and one of the best places on the planet to watch them turns out to be the Niagara River in November and December. Fourteen gull species have been seen here in one day, which is a world record. And since this seemingly blah time of year is sandwiched between the beautiful fall colours of October and the snowy blankets of January, birders often flock to the river to see what they can find.

Starting at the mouth of the river in Niagara-on-the-Lake, ease into identification by looking for the three most common species of gulls at this time: the herring gull, ring-billed gull and Bonaparte's gull. This is a great place to watch for other birds, too, such as red-throated loons, long-tailed ducks and horned grebes.

Travelling up the river by car, there are many stops to make. At Queenston, scan the flocks of gulls for a little gull

(the world's smallest gull is the size of a mourning dove) or a great black-backed gull (the world's largest gull, it's the size of a turkey vulture). The overlook at Adam Beck Power Dam is a wonderful place to look down at the flying gulls, and the identification of Arctic species such as the glaucous gull or Iceland gull is much easier.

At Niagara Falls, peer through the mist and see if you can find a usually oceanic species such as a black-legged kittiwake or a Sabine's gull. Above the Falls, scan through resting gulls to look for a lesser black-backed gull or Thayer's gull. Carefully check the rocks here for a purple sandpiper, and take a look at all the different duck species as well. All along your river-edge travels, watch for southern Ontario specialty birds such as the black vulture, tufted titmouse, Carolina wren and northern mockingbird. And remember, Niagara is a perfect place to shake away those November birder blahs.

↑ **Where's Waldo: Can you find the one lesser black-backed gull in this resting flock?**

Short Hills Provincial Park

A rich supply of streams and valleys has spawned habitat diversity in this small, stunning provincial park

What Makes This Hot Spot Hot?

- An impressive variety of habitats across the park support high biodiversity and make for a fascinating day hike.
- Endless streams and trails allow visitors to explore the park in great depth.
- The main artery of the park is the only cold-water stream system in Niagara and is said to be the cleanest in the region.

Address: Short Hills Provincial Park, P.O. Box 158, Dunnville, ON N1A 2X5
Tel.: (905) 774-6642
Website: friendsofshorthillspark.ca

Open year-round

Adjacent to the town of Pelham and the city of St. Catharines, Short Hills Provincial Park offers visitors respite from life's hustle and bustle. Part of the Fonthill Kame Moraine, the area was once scoured by glaciers, strewn with deposits of sand, gravel and clay and flooded during the Wisconsin Ice Age. Today, the 660-hectare-parkland features a complex network of remnant streams left by retreating glacial waters. Over time, these streams have carved valleys, canyons and the short hills for which the park is named. Small gorges and floodplains throughout drain into nearby Twelve Mile Creek.

Part of southern Ontario's Carolinian Forest Region, Short Hills is home to a host of such rare species as sassafras and black gum trees, but it is also a welcoming home to mammals, from coyotes, white-tailed deer and red foxes, a wide range of bird species, including the great horned owl, bobolink and scarlet tanager,

and amphibians and reptiles.

Once you access the park from one of three entrances, the area's sheer habitat diversity becomes immediately apparent. In a matter of just 15 minutes, you might enjoy the scent of a planted pine forest, glimpse frogs and turtles in a floodplain swamp, walk through an old-growth forest and then find yourself in a meadow vibrating with insects. The marked trails are as widespread as the park's dozens of streams, so be sure to grab a camera and visit either Swayze Falls or one of several other cascades.

Twelve Mile Creek, the main artery of the park, is the only cold-water stream in all of the Niagara Region. Fed by cold groundwater that originates from glacial formations, it boasts the highest water-quality grading and highest benthic invertebrate diversity of any creek within Niagara. The crisp and clear waters are also home to the only self-sustained brook trout population in the area.

←↑ A network of streams, valleys, wetland and trails, this park hosts tree species from the Carolinian forest as well as a wide variety of wildlife.

Wainfleet Bog Conservation Area

Feel the peat bounce beneath your feet as you trek through a remarkable bog ecosystem

What Makes This Hot Spot Hot?

- There's an appreciable diversity of both vascular and non-vascular plants, some of which are subarctic species.
- It's home to an isolated population of the eastern Massasauga rattlesnake.
- Experience the unfamiliar scenery and outstanding biodiversity of a unique bog, the southernmost of its kind in Canada.

Address: 20389 Erie Peat Road, Wainfleet, ON
Tel.: (905) 788-3135, Ext. 258 (Conservation Areas Supervisor)
Websites: npca.ca/conservation-areas/wainfleet-bog; ontariotrails.on.ca/trails/view/wainfleet-bog-trail

Open year-round

Visitors to the Wainfleet Bog Conservation Area can look forward to a spongy walk over ancient history, even if that history is young in geologic time. As glaciers from the last ice age melted some 12,000 years ago, water pooled in this low, flat land. Trapped by the Onondaga Escarpment and unable to drain south into Lake Erie, the standing water gradually nurtured plants that could tolerate an acidic environment with low nutrients. A perpetual cycle of growth and death left behind layers of decomposed organic matter that tell their own story—and explain the dip and rebound you'll feel underfoot when walking the bog's trails.

Today's bog represents the boundary of the southernmost bog ecosystem of its type in Canada. After a century of extensive peat mining, drainage and agriculture, the Wainfleet Bog, at 1,200 hectares, is a fraction of its original 20,000-hectare land mass. A rare habitat in southern Ontario, the bog is notable for the biodiversity of its flora and fauna. A fortunate visitor may spot an eastern Massasauga rattlesnake sunning on the forest floor—the bog protects an isolated population of Ontario's only venomous snake. Worry not—these animals are timid and would rather hide or rattle than strike.

The conservation area itself covers 801 hectares, and visitors reach it via a gravel road. Two linear trails allow access into the bog from the parking lot, but the majority of the property is thick and uninterrupted. On a warm spring or summer day, it feels humid and moist, a little like being in a tropical jungle. Wild swaths of waterlogged forest and scrub remain unseen and untouched by people. Reptile and amphibian enthusiasts are delighted to find that there are potentially 25 species at home here. Grab your binoculars and experience the rush overhead of migrating birds, or look closely at the ground to see bog plants such as Labrador tea, leatherleaf, cotton leaf and carnivorous sundew.

↑ A boardwalk takes visitors over an especially wet area in this rare southern Ontario bog.

↖ These trumpet lichens are perfectly at home in a shady bog habitat.

Woodend Conservation Area

This stand of Carolinian forest offers visitors a sweeping view of the neighbourhood's biodiversity

What Makes This Hot Spot Hot?

- There are excellent passerine birding opportunities, views of Lake Ontario and stunning sunsets.
- The escarpment habitat acts as a stronghold for many Carolinian plant and animal species.
- Woodend offers respite from the intense human development that has grown up around it.

Address: Woodend Conservation Area, Taylor Road, Niagara-on-the-Lake, ON
Tel.: (905) 788-3135
Website: npca.ca/conservation-areas/woodend

Open year-round

↗ **Watch for the spotted salamander in the forest leaf litter.**

Woodend Conservation Area offers a graphic lesson in the Earth's history, but be sure to take a moment to appreciate its human history as well. Originally granted as farmland to United Empire Loyalist Peter Lampman during the American Revolutionary War, this spot saw its share of action during the War of 1812. Perched atop the Niagara Escarpment and located mere miles from military clashes at Queenston Heights, Beaver Dams and Lundy's Lane, the property proved to be a perfect observation point for armies from both sides. Today, visitors can peaceably enjoy the sweeping views of the escarpment slopes and forests and the meadows below.

This conservation area can be thoroughly explored in under two hours. A trail system allows visitors to hike the escarpment's base, mid-section and top rim, thanks to a section of Canada's longest and oldest footpath, the Bruce Trail. As you hike up from the base, take note of the conspicuous rock strata, a literal reminder that you are retracing geological history, step by step. The escarpment creates an invaluable wildlife corridor, and standing at the top, you can watch white-tailed deer graze

in the adjacent field. Woodend's green space enhances the health of the artificial wetlands along its northwest boundary and provides habitat for creatures like the spotted salamander, which marches down the hillside every spring to find water in which to breed.

Note how the surrounding hardwood trees dominate the escarpment slopes. Passerines frequent the layers of this forest, making the area attractive with birdwatchers. It's also a popular playground for hikers, cross-country skiers and photographers, while students and educators at nearby elementary schools and Niagara College as well as scientists and nature-loving citizens use the conservation area as a classroom and backyard laboratory. Generations from all walks of life have visited Woodend, burnishing its reputation as a natural treasure.

↑ Sections of Woodend are cloaked in green from the dense forest canopy overhead to the lush forest floor.

Algonquin
Provincial
Park

(2)

Petawawa

Pembroke

(21)

(41)

(10) (19)

(60) Eganville

(4)

Barry's Bay

Renfrew

(9)

Ottawa

★

(417)

(5)

Nepean

(15)

Almonte

(416)

(62)

(28)

Bancroft

(3)

Perth

Smiths Falls

(41)

(7)

(29)

(7)

Westport

Brockville

(62)

(8)

(17)

Madoc

(13)

(6)

Tweed

(20)

(41)

(37)

Napanee

(14)

(401)

Belleville

(12)

Kingston

(1)

Trenton

(11)

(16)

N

W   E

S

118

(18)

Eastern Ontario

Amherst Island

The winter owl capital of Canada

What Makes This Hot Spot Hot?

- Depending on the year, Amherst Island is one of the best places to see owls anywhere in the country.
- Hawks, eagles, falcons and shrikes can be found here too.
- Open areas allow you to see these birds hunt, rest and perhaps even interact with each other.

Address: Ferry dock at Millhaven
Tel.: N/A
Website: kingstonfieldnaturalists.org/birding/amherst_island.pdf

Ferry runs year-round (amherstisland.on.ca/ferry.htm)

↗ **Cold feet are not an issue for this snowy owl.**

Whether a result of a plentiful food source of voles or the vast fields whose edges offer this predator protective cover, Amherst Island is the place to see winter owls. Just west of Kingston, the roughly 6,600-hectare island is made up of mostly agricultural land interspersed with wooded areas and marshes, and 10 species of Ontario owl have been recorded here.

Some owl species go through what are called irruption cycles, which means that in certain winters—possibly as a result of a lack of food on their normal wintering grounds—owls leave northern areas en masse and can be found in southern Ontario. These years are perfect for an Amherst visit, though this Lake Ontario island welcomes at least some owls every year. On a winter birding day, arrive at Millhaven early to board the ferry (check online for the current schedule). Keep an eye out for winter ducks in the ice-free ferry channel, and scan for white-winged

gull species such as the Iceland gull or glaucous gull.

Once on the island, explore the country roads by car, roaming as far afield as you have time for. Most of Amherst Island is privately owned, but there is no need to leave the public roads to see these birds. Watch for a fence post that seems unusually tall—that extra height may actually be a perching short-eared owl. On the white fields and shoreline ice, watch for lumpy irregularities—these might be snowy owls. You may also see other raptorial birds such as red-tailed hawks, rough-legged hawks and northern shrikes.

Leave time to take a hike in Owl Woods on the eastern part of the island. Depending on the year, this is where to watch for species such as the northern saw-whet, boreal, long-eared, barred and maybe even a great gray owl. Some of these owls hide and sleep in the forest conifers during the day, so take care to view them from a distance. Keep your voice low, and enjoy a true nature experience.

↑ A short-eared owl on Amherst Island employs a sit-and-wait hunting strategy on a roadside fence post.

Barron Canyon

On the rugged east side of Algonquin, where stalwart pines and hard-edged granite rule

What Makes This Hot Spot Hot?

- One of Ontario's two signature canyons, Barron Canyon is steeper and narrower than northwestern Ontario's Ouimet Canyon.
- The views from the cliff top and from a paddler's perspective offer two radically different experiences.
- Unusual birds and plants make this inhospitable habitat their home.

Address: Km 29.0 of the Barron Canyon Road, Algonquin Provincial Park, ON
Tel.: (705) 633-5572 (Algonquin Provincial Park, General Inquiry)
Website: ontariotrails.on.ca/trails/view/barron-canyon-trail

Open year-round

Ontario's dramatic geological history is responsible for virtually all of the province's impressive vistas, but for those of us who revel in a view from on high, a hike along the Barron Canyon Trail, on the eastern edge of Algonquin Park, is not to be missed. The 1.5-kilometre loop trail leads to the canyon's unfenced north rim, where you should take a deep breath and be sure of your footing before gazing down to the Barron River some 100 metres below.

As you do, consider what led to this remarkable scene. Billions of years ago, the sandy deposits that eventually hardened into the Canadian Shield lay beneath an ancient sea. When a shift in tectonic plates thrust the limestone cap upward, it shattered into fault lines that ran from the northwest to the southeast. Fast-forward millions of centuries to the massive meltwaters created when the ice sheets of the last ice age beat a dramatic retreat north. Water finds the lowest point, which is just what happened when the waters of the vast post-glacial Lake Algonquin carved their way through the fault line that is now the Barron Canyon. In a mere few centuries, a torrent that scientists have

↙→ At Barron Canyon, the views are equally compelling, whether from the river or from on high.

described as equivalent to a thousand Niagaras resolved itself as today's comparatively peaceful Barron River and, later, as the Mattawa and Ottawa Rivers to the north.

Barron Canyon's towering cliffs provide nesting areas for the barn swallow, eastern phoebe, raven and red-tailed hawk, while the yellow-bellied flycatcher, northern water-thrush and common yellow-throat make their home on the wooded canyon slopes. The calcium-rich rock crevices are a supportive habitat for unusual plants such as maidenhair spleenwort, bulblet fern and mountain woodsia.

As wondrous as the canyon is from above, however, those on the river wax poetic about the spectacle from water level. Canoeists paddling quietly in the shadow of the steep, lichen-encrusted cliffs inevitably describe a journey through a primeval landscape. A lone bald eagle silently soaring overhead completes the picture.

Bon Echo Provincial Park

French for 'good echo,' Bon Echo was named for the effects of its most prominent feature: the towering and formidable Mazinaw Rock

What Makes This Hot Spot Hot?

- Bon Echo features one of Canada's best indigenous pictograph sites.
- Abundant wildlife, including rare species that take advantage of cliff habitats, make the park their home.
- There are plentiful hiking, paddling, wildlife viewing and photo opportunities.

Address: 16151 Hwy 41
Cloyne, ON K0H 1K0
Tel.: (613) 336-2228
Website: ontarioparks.com/park/bonecho

Open mid-May to mid-October

↗ **Meet Ontario's only lizard: the five-lined skink.**

At 100 metres tall and 1.5 kilometres long, Mazinaw Rock dominates the landscape of Bon Echo Provincial Park. Formed by volcanic activity and glaciation, the rock plunges to a depth of 145 metres in Mazinaw Lake. This geological colossus has long captured the attention of campers, paddlers and daring climbers and is the reason the area was first established as a tourist destination in the late 1800s. Long before European settlement, though, Mazinaw was an important place for the area's indigenous inhabitants.

To view one of the largest rock art sites in Canada, rent a canoe or take an interpretive tour on the park's boat, a 26-passenger cruise vessel named *The Wanderer*. Mazinaw Rock is adorned with more than 260 Aboriginal pictographs, believed to have been painted by the Algonquin people. The word Mazinaw itself comes from the Algonquin language, meaning, roughly, "painted rock." Rendered in red ochre, the paintings depict animals, humans, geographic forms and abstract symbols. Their

age has not been established.

Humans are not the only creatures drawn to Mazinaw Rock—interesting wildlife species also take advantage of the unique landform. Peregrine falcons nest here and can be seen circling overhead or plummeting to the water as they hunt for an unsuspecting duck or gull. Ontario's only lizard—the five-lined skink—also lives here, sheltered among the moss and broken rocks that litter the exposed Canadian Shield. An abundance of other wildlife calls the park home, and the keen observer will not be disappointed.

Bon Echo Provincial Park is perfect for a day visit but also provides camping facilities, from fully serviced to back-country. Hiking trails range from 1 to 17 kilometres, including the spectacular Cliff Top Trail, which provides stunning views of the park. Paddling may be the best way to see Bon Echo, however, and it allows visitors to share perspective with the First Nations and Europeans who came before.

⬆ **Cliffs rise majestically from Bon Echo's Mazinaw Lake.**

Bonnechere Caves

Step into a time machine on the shores of the Bonnechere River

What Makes This Hot Spot Hot?

- The Bonnechere Caves are one of the best examples in North America of a solution cave—created when acidic groundwater dissolves the stone.
- The scalloped walls are a veritable library of ancient marine-life fossils.
- The caves are situated near one of the prettiest waterfalls in the area.

Address: 1237 Fourth Chute Road, Eganville, ON K0J 1T0
Tel.: (613) 628-2283
Website: bonnecherecaves.com

Open daily from the Victoria Day weekend through September 30; weekends until Thanksgiving

Long before the Bonnechere Caves existed, much of North America, including what is now the Ottawa Valley, was bathed in the waters of a warm, tropical sea. Some 450 million years ago, the Ordovician Period was characterized by the intense diversification of marine animals—fish and other creatures with backbones were not quite on the evolutionary horizon, but the sea teemed with invertebrate life. The period ended with a mass extinction, but thanks to the blankets of sediment the sea had deposited over time, some of these marine animals were perfectly preserved as fossils.

Let's speed through the rough ride the continent endured before the last ice age, about 10,000 years ago. As glaciers melted and retreated from the limestone that underlies the Ottawa Valley,

↙→ **Boardwalks lead visitors through a sculpted interior created over thousands of years by acidic groundwaters.**

the landscape as we know it today—lakes, rivers and rolling hills—eventually took shape. The carbonic acid present in moving groundwater can dissolve bedrock over time, and as water flowed along the course of what is now the Bonnechere River, it worked its magic on the limestone riverbed. After thousands of years, the caves emerged—not carved away by the brutal action of grinding glaciers but, instead, "melted" away by the acidic groundwater.

The privately managed Bonnechere Caves are a dark, damp habitat, perhaps made even more mysterious for that. As we gaze upon the dramatically sculpted walls, where the fossils of generations of ancient sea creatures have been captured in perpetuity, it's hard not to be entranced by what time has fashioned. Once you've explored the caves, come out into the sunlit present and visit the Fourth Chute, a beautiful cascading waterfall on the Bonnechere River.

Britannia Conservation Area

An urban nature oasis with rich wetlands and towering woodlands, this is Ottawa's premier birding hot spot

What Makes This Hot Spot Hot?

- At this accessible urban nature oasis, visitors can explore a variety of habitats.
- Britannia offers excellent birding, particularly during migration seasons.
- This conservation area is a convenient side trip for Ottawa visitors and residents alike.

Address: Main access to trails is via Cassels Street, east of Britannia Road
Tel.: N/A
Website: ottawa.ca/en/residents/water-and-environment/air-land-and-water/conservation-areas-forests-and-parks

Open year-round

↗ **The water-loving mink makes a snowy appearance in wintertime Britannia.**

Situated on a peninsula at a narrowing in the Ottawa River, Britannia Conservation Area is tucked conveniently within Ottawa's urban space. At just 79 hectares in size, it supports surprising biodiversity and is noteworthy for the number of bird species that have been found here. At its core lies Mud Lake. This large pond abounds with aquatic vegetation, holds various turtle species and attracts a variety of waterfowl. Towering woodlands and wet thickets surround it on three sides, creating lovely landscapes, especially during the fall. Some regionally scarce woody plant species also thrive here. To the west, the forest melds into brushy habitat, and the Ottawa River provides an ever-present if not always obvious backdrop.

A visit to Britannia should first include the view of Mud Lake from Cassels Street along the pond's north edge. From this vantage point, it's possible to see and photograph resident

↑ **A view of Mud Lake's aquatic vegetation.**

wildlife such as wood ducks, beavers and mink. Access the woods beyond by a network of dog-free trails from the pond's northwest corner. The flat and easy trail begins in younger woodland and eventually enters a mature forest dominated by lofty white pines, sugar maples and red oaks. A couple of lookout points along the pond's west side provide a chance to spot skulking herons and other pond wildlife; footpaths leading away from the lake's west side bring you to open, brushy habitats.

Bird lovers may wish to climb the trail that leads up the limestone ridge on the north side of Cassels Street. On a good day during spring or fall migration, an abundance of songbirds may pass in the shrubbery at eye level. Waterfowl, wading birds and gulls fly overhead as they transit to and from the Ottawa River. From here, you can also descend to the river below for a clearer view of the untamed Deschênes Rapids.

Elbow Lake Environmental Education Centre

A learning hot spot in the Frontenac Arch Natural Area

What Makes This Hot Spot Hot?

- You'll discover an outdoor classroom in one of the region's most beautiful settings.
- The ELEEC offers an on-the-ground education in how to protect and preserve our natural heritage. Download the Elbow Lake Trail Guide interpretive app at elbowlakecentre.ca/app
- It's a meeting place where like-minded educational and conservation organizations can forge partnerships.

Address: 1500 Hewlett-Packard Lane, Perth Road, ON K0H 2L0
Tel.: (613) 353-7968
Website: elbowlakecentre.ca

Open year-round; contact ELEEC for details or to register your intent to visit

Ontario has an abundance of wilderness spaces where the public is encouraged to explore the natural world. While a good number provide a helping educational hand via interpretive centres and signage, not too many exist exclusively to teach the value of understanding, appreciating and preserving our ecosystems. One that does, however, is the Elbow Lake Environmental Education Centre (ELEEC) north of Kingston, in eastern Ontario.

The ELEEC lies within conservation lands owned and managed by the Nature Conservancy of Canada as the Frontenac Arch Natural Area. A southerly extension of the Canadian Shield, the Frontenac Arch links the northern boreal forest with the forests of the Adirondack and Appalachian Mountains to the south. It's a rugged landscape studded with cliffs, outcroppings,

lakes and rivers, woodlands and wetlands. It is also one of the most concentrated areas of biodiversity in Canada.

A true living classroom, the ELEEC serves as the primary outreach site for the nearby Queen's University Biological Station and is located on roughly 470 hectares and six kilometres of shoreline on Elbow, Spectacle and Upper Rock Lakes. Much of that is a nature reserve, but the ELEEC's

trail system allows access to habitats where southern species such as the shagbark hickory, the southern flying squirrel and the Allegheny vine live in harmony with such northerly denizens as the tamarack and the snowshoe hare. The ELEEC is also home to endangered species such as the butternut tree and at-risk species that include the cerulean warbler and the Blanding's turtle.

The ELEEC offers lively educational events, seminars and workshops for adults and families, as well as programs for area secondary schools. It also plays a role in creating the next generation of naturalists by giving kids an unforgettable summer adventure at its Eco-Adventure Day Camp. A common space and cabins are available to groups keen to hold conferences, meetings or classes in one of Ontario's finest wilderness spots.

↑ A morning mist lingers over the Frontenac Arch's Elbow Lake.

← An overcast day at the ELEEC beaver pond.

Foley Mountain Conservation Area

After enjoying the big views, search for small wildlife

What Makes This Hot Spot Hot?

- There are wonderful views from Spy Rock.
- Take advantage of the extensive Rideau Trail system while you're here.
- Find fungi, caterpillars and dragonfly nymphs along the many trails and pond edges.

Address: 105 Perth Road North, Westport, ON K0G 1X0
Tel.: (613) 273-3255
Website: rvca.ca/careas/foley

Open year-round

↗ A fallen log festooned with turkey tail fungus at Foley Mountain.

Foley Mountain Conservation Area, near the town of Westport in eastern Ontario, is a little place with a big view. On top of this granite ridge, you'll find the Spy Rock lookout, which offers a glorious panoramic perspective of the town, the Upper Rideau Lake and the surrounding area. Traversing the area's 323 hectares is a series of short trails that allow you to explore forests and ponds. The Rideau Trail, a 387-kilometre network of trails linking Kingston and Ottawa, also passes through.

Foley Mountain is part of the Frontenac Arch, an hourglass-shaped piece of the Canadian Shield that connects the northern boreal forests to those of the Adirondack and Appalachian Mountains. The St. Lawrence River Valley intersects the Frontenac Arch from west to east, bringing forests from the Great Lakes and Atlantic regions into play as well. The area has long served as a wildlife corridor, but artifacts found here indicate that it also did service as a human highway, a meeting

place for indigenous residents from many eastern North America regions in search of trading opportunities.

After taking in the big picture from Spy Rock, why not focus on some of the small things along the trails? The mixed-forest trees and associated herbaceous plants provide food for the caterpillars of many butterfly and moth species. Keep an eye peeled for the impressively hairy giant leopard moth caterpillar. Hunt around the pond shorelines for a myriad of modestly sized aquatic creatures—dragonfly nymphs, giant water bugs, whirligig beetles, waterboatmen and backswimmers.

Foley Mountain is also a fruitful place in which to look for fungi. One group, the bracket fungi, are well represented here and includes species such as turkey tail, tinder polypore and artist's conk. An important part of every Ontario ecosystem, fungi are amazingly diverse and beautiful—getting to know the hundreds of different species is a challenging but rewarding naturalist pursuit.

↑ From Spy Rock, there's a wonderful view of the much-loved historic town of Westport.

Frontenac Provincial Park

A wilderness playground where geological eras clash and paddlers, hikers and campers savour an ecological sweet spot

What Makes This Hot Spot Hot?

- This park boasts a rich diversity of plant, bird, mammal, snake and butterfly and dragonfly species.
- For those who want to rent canoes and other gear, Frontenac Outfitters is located just outside the park gates.
- Half an hour north of Kingston, Frontenac Park is Canadian Shield country at its best—and much more.

Address: P.O. Box 11, 6700 Salmon Lake Road, Sydenham, ON K0H 2T0
Tel.: (613) 376-3489
Website: frontenacpark.ca

Open year-round

↗ **A great blue heron wades through a Frontenac marsh in full bloom.**

Four seasons of the year, eastern Ontarians are fiercely loyal to Frontenac Provincial Park, with good reason. This park has something for every outdoor lover. A half-hour drive north of Kingston, Frontenac sits on the southernmost edge of the Canadian Shield in an area known as the Frontenac Arch. At the confluence of five forest regions in eastern Ontario, the Arch links the boreal forest of the Canadian Shield in the north to the forests of the Adirondack and Appalachian Mountains to the south. The landform is a dramatic interruption of the otherwise flat countryside of southern Ontario. And what an interruption: A remarkable melding of north and south, it's a landscape of forests and lakes, wetlands and rugged cliffs formed from exposed Precambrian rock.

Frontenac embraces 5,355 hectares of this wild area. Dotted with 22 lakes and bordered by an additional six, the park draws paddlers eager to experience a range of canoe routes—some explore the classic deep, clear, cold, low-vegetation lakes of the Shield; others lead to more

southerly examples of warm, shallow, weedy bodies of water. Hikers, too, enjoy a surfeit of choice, with more than 100 kilometres of interconnected trails, while for geology fans, the park represents a rich banquet. During the last ice age, glacial activity carved out a system of alternating ridges and valleys in this region, and all across the park is evidence of the unmistakable impact of mile-thick continental ice sheets scraping away bedrock and soil and polishing and radically resculpting billion-year-old Precambrian rocks.

A transition zone between the ranges for northern and southern plants, Frontenac nurtures some 700 species—almost half of the plant life found in Ontario. An estimated 50 locally important sites support rare species of ferns, sedges, mosses and orchids. Roughly 25 species of mammals make the park their home, from the tiny, plentiful voles and shrews to the white-tailed deer, black bear and moose. In the woodland and wetlands and along lakeshores, more than 170 bird species, including the rarely seen red-shouldered hawk, can be found.

↑ Sun-warmed rock on the edge of Birch Lake.

↖ A patch of blue sky lingers during sunset on Kingsford Lake, at the park's northwest border.

Gillies Grove

A forest wonderland shelters the province's tallest white pine

What Makes This Hot Spot Hot?

- Wildflowers, birds and small mammals populate this protected woodlot.
- On the outskirts of a small Ontario town, this old-growth forest survived the regional industry.
- The tallest white pine in Ontario grows here.

Address: 412 Gillies Grove Road, Arnprior, ON K7S 0A1
Tel.: N/A
Website: mfnc.ca/gilliesgrove

Open year-round

Not every child can take a shortcut to school through a stand of one of the last remaining old-growth forests in Canada, but in Arnprior, it's one of the perks of living near Gillies Grove.

Once the address of a local lumber baron, this mixed forest sits on the town's north corner, a little beyond where the Ottawa and Madawaska Rivers famously meet. Somehow, a stand of white pines nestled in the woodlot evaded the axe and sawmills that fuelled the town's early economy, and today, the property is designated a National Historic Site of Canada. On site is a Colonial Revival-style house built in 1937 with white pine from this very land and recognized for the role it plays in the region's human history. But it is the remarkable natural attributes of Gillies Grove itself that draw residents and visitors alike.

The Grove, as it is known locally, offers peace and renewal year-round. In spring, as the leaves of the mixed forest of sugar maple, yellow

A scarlet tanager offers a summertime splash of colour in the leafy-green environment of Gillies Grove.

→ Gillies Grove: Home to the tallest white pine in Ontario.

birch, American beech and basswood trees emerge, the forest floor is carpeted with red and white trilliums. During summer, the green canopy offers a cooling escape from the sun. A scarlet tanager might flit overhead as a red-shouldered hawk seeks a perch high in the towering pines. In autumn, the deciduous trees burst into colour, eventually littering the paths with leaves. Once the snow falls, the natural quiet of the forest may be interrupted by the sound of a pileated woodpecker loudly searching for a meal.

At the heart of Gillies Grove is a towering example of the white pines that were once clear-cut for ship masts and lumber. At 47 metres, it has been designated the tallest white pine in Ontario by the Nature Conservancy of Canada. It's true that no ecosystem stands still, but let's hope that a few more generations have a chance to appreciate the story this mighty giant tells.

Lake Doré

At this eastern Ontario lake, birders have come to expect the unexpected

What Makes This Hot Spot Hot?

- Spring and fall migrants include large numbers of waterfowl and gulls.
- A wide range of different bird species can be seen around the lake's perimeter.
- From a canoe launched from Biederman Park, you can watch for common loons, common terns and osprey.

Address: Eight kilometres north of Eganville, on the west side of Hwy 41.
Tel.: N/A
Website: ottawavalley. travel/naturalist-guide/ destinations/7-lake-dore- shaw-woods-and-pond

Open year-round

↗ **This long-tailed duck will briefly flash its long tail feather before disappearing under the water on a fishing expedition.**

At roughly eight kilometres long and five kilometres wide, this pretty lake in eastern Ontario, several kilometres north of Eganville, is the largest lake in North America without an island. Lake Doré is an extremely popular destination for birds—and birdwatchers. Indeed, Lake Doré birders in the know expect the unexpected. That denizen of the Arctic, the Sabine's gull? And the rarely seen little gull? Both have been spotted here.

The uninterrupted surface of the lake makes for an impressive canvas, with sweeping sightlines on the water as well as in the sky overhead. For those who want to get closer to the action, there are three public boat launches on the lake. But a spotting scope on shore should allow you to see much of what you want to see, including the surprises.

Waterfowl and gulls start arriving when the ice breaks up in April, and the lake is a staging area for migrants until late May. Mallards, common mergansers, common goldeneyes and ring-billed gulls and herring gulls soon touch down

↑ **Summer clouds are perfectly reflected in the island-free waters of Lake Doré.**

as well. These are followed by ring-necked ducks and buffleheads. Horned grebes and red-necked grebes are scarce in spring, but by September and October, they appear in healthy numbers, when northern sea ducks are also in evidence. Flocks of brant geese have been seen in mid-May and are not unheard of in October.

Bald eagles are also on the lake, but at the weedy west end, where pike and bass linger in the shallow water,

watch out for that great fishing bird, the osprey. If the timing is right, you might spy one soaring overhead before dramatically dropping, feet first, to take its catch.

↖↑ **A great fishing bird, the osprey watches the shallow waters from above before dropping down to snatch up a dinner of northern pike.**

Lake on the Mountain

On the edge of Lake Ontario, nature's own infinity pool

What Makes This Hot Spot Hot?

- A short drive from the Glenora Ferry, Lake on the Mountain is the perfect introduction to the wonders of Prince Edward County.
- It's a chance to stand on a piece of the county's geological history.
- The park here affords a remarkable view of the surrounding area.

Address: 296 County Road 7, Picton, ON K0K 2T0
Tel.: (613) 393-3319
Website: en.wikipedia. org/wiki/Lake_on_the_ Mountain_Provincial_Park

Day use only from mid-May through mid-October

↗ A dramatic 60-metre drop separates the inland waters of Lake on the Mountain from the Bay of Quinte below.

As the mile-thick glaciers of the last ice age retreated to the north, an irregularly shaped headland emerged at the eastern end of what is now Lake Ontario. Today, that headland is known as Prince Edward County, a bucolic landscape that features limestone-plain habitats called alvars, rocky outcroppings, rolling fields and, on the southwestern shore, the world's largest freshwater sandbar and dune system.

Underpinning the entire region, some 250 metres down, is the ancient Precambrian rock that forms the Canadian Shield. For the most part buried in southern Ontario, it occasionally makes an appearance aboveground in the county, the most famous example being the Amherstburg Inlier. One respected area naturalist has likened the county's shape to that of a "lopsided layer cake." And, indeed, at the county's north and east borders, the topography is notably different than on the shores of Sandbanks. A

plateau of limestone gradually rises, eventually reaching more than 75 metres in height. On this plateau, you'll find one of Prince Edward County's more curious physical features.

At a height of some 60 metres, Lake on the Mountain is a freshwater lake that sits on the edge of this limestone plateau, with views of the Bay of Quinte and the Adolphus Reach. While a short strip of horizontal ground separates the shorelines of Lake Ontario and the modest Lake on the Mountain, there is a dramatic vertical drop between the two bodies of water. Legends abound about how the 34-metre-deep lake came to be, but the most reliable scientific explanation is that it is the product of a collapsed doline, which occurred when a cave made of carbonate limestone rock was gradually eroded by underground springs. After thousands of years, the cave roof collapsed, leaving behind a basin that filled with water to become Lake on the Mountain.

↑ **Small, placid Lake on the Mountain sits on a plateau of limestone.**

Lemoine Point Conservation Area

Eastern Ontario's largest publicly accessible tract of wooded Lake Ontario shoreline

What Makes This Hot Spot Hot?

- There are stunning views of Lake Ontario from the area's shoreline trails.
- Well-groomed trails and picnic areas are perfect for family outings.
- You'll encounter exceedingly friendly bird residents and a bay dotted with tundra swans, long-tailed ducks and gulls.

Address: 1441 Coverdale Drive, Kingston, ON
Tel.: (613) 546-4228
Website: crca.ca/conservation-lands/conservation-areas/lemoine-point-conservation-area

Open year-round

Residents of Greater Kingston are spoiled for choice when it comes to access to protected wildlands, but Lemoine Point Conservation Area is an especially treasured destination. The Cataraqui Region Conservation Authority (CRCA) describes it as the last large, publicly accessible tract of wooded Lake Ontario shoreline in the region. It's impossible for city dwellers not to appreciate the splendour of this gift.

Tucked between Lake Ontario and Collins Bay, the point features 136 hectares of mixed forest, field and marsh, as well as more than 2,500 metres of spectacular waterfront. The area is part of the Frontenac Arch Biosphere—the ancient granite bridge that stretches from the Canadian Shield to the Adirondack Mountains, recognized in 2002 as a UNESCO World Biosphere Reserve for its rich natural environment and history. That legacy is fully realized at Lemoine Point.

Gorgeous four seasons of the year, Lemoine Point has 11 kilometres of gently rolling trails that lead through a mixed forest of towering trees and dappled light. In early spring, the paths are bordered with thousands of trilliums; by summer, other wildflowers have taken over, and the mature canopy offers shade and respite to walkers of all ages. In fall, the deciduous leaves flame against a brilliant blue sky; and in winter, hikers, dog walkers and cross-country skiers amicably share the trails. Year-round, black-capped chickadees can be fed by hand with treats of sunflower seeds; occasionally, a downy woodpecker may get in on the action.

There are two entranceways to Lemoine Point. One is at the end of Front Road, just past the city airport, a route that bypasses the bucolic farmland still owned by a descendant of the Coverdale family, who donated the point to the CRCA. The other is off Highway 33.

←↑ **The last, large, publicly accessible tract of wooded Lake Ontario shoreline, Lemoine Point is a nature wonderland with wide, groomed trails.**

Lennox & Addington County Dark Sky Viewing Area

Eastern Ontarians are reclaiming their starry, starry nights

What Makes This Hot Spot Hot?

- It's the most southerly point in Ontario where observing the night sky is still an option.
- Visitors can view the stars without optical aids, but a pair of binoculars makes it that much better.
- It's within a comfortable driving distance of a handful of midsized eastern Ontario cities and many towns.

Address: 7980 County Road 41, Erinsville, ON K0K 2A0
Tel.: N/A
Website: lennox-addington. on.ca/must-see/dark-sky-viewing-area.html

Open year-round

As a five-year-old, Canada's best-known astronomy writer, Terence Dickinson, recalls looking up at the dark night sky and seeing the Milky Way from his Toronto backyard. That was back in the early 1950s, but it's an experience a star-curious, city-dwelling youngster is far less likely to enjoy today. We Earthlings have managed to spoil quite a lot of our natural world at ground level. But we've also blotted out the stars above with the fog of artificial lights from communities all across the country. As a result, amateur astronomers in southern Ontario have been prevented from pursuing an all-consuming hobby unless they drive many hours from home.

In eastern Ontario, the night sky has opened up again, thanks to Dickinson. Working with Lennox & Addington County personnel, the

founding editor of *SkyNews*, Canada's only astronomy magazine, spearheaded a project that would exploit what has been described as eastern Ontario's "inland dark sky peninsula." It's a sparsely populated area—and thus devoid of light pollution—extending southeast from Algonquin Provincial Park to roughly 40 kilometres north of Napanee.

For an endeavour that involves looking at objects 100,000 light-years away, the requirements are remarkably simple. The Lennox & Addington County Dark Sky Viewing Area, located at the most southerly point in Ontario where the night sky is still pristine, includes a large concrete pad for camera or telescope setup or the placement of lawn chairs for viewing. There's a parking area, interpretive signage and a washroom, all maintained year-round. A dark sky overhead completes the picture. The site is a 30-minute drive from the intersection of Hwy 401 and Hwy 41, which runs from Napanee to Pembroke, in Renfrew County, a few hours' north. Open since 2012, the viewing area has given astrophotographers and astronomers new opportunities to see what's been out there all along.

←↑ Astrophotography from an eastern Ontario dark sky viewing area brilliantly captures the star-studded Milky Way.

Little Cataraqui Creek Conservation Area

A reclaimed swath of farmland offers year-round access to the natural world

What Makes This Hot Spot Hot?

- An elaborate network of trails and boardwalks allows for first-hand sightings of birds and small mammals.
- Little Cat is built for wintertime activities for the whole family.
- In summer, recreational opportunities include hiking and paddling.

Address: 1641 Perth Road (Division Street), Kingston, ON K0H 1S0
Tel.: (613) 546-4228
Website: crca.ca/conservation-lands/conservation-areas/little-cataraqui-creek-conservation-area

Open year-round

A sprawling 394-hectare site featuring marsh, field and forest habitat, Little Cataraqui Creek Conservation Area was conceived almost a half century ago by the Cataraqui Region Conservation Authority to manage local water flow. Little Cat, as it is affectionately known, started life as a patchwork of retired farmlands north of Kingston that was transformed by a reservoir and dam. Today, it is one of Greater Kingston's most popular outdoor recreation facilities.

A year-round activity centre for nature appreciation and recreation, Little Cat truly hums in the winter months. In fact, its 13 kilometres of groomed cross-country ski and snowshoe trails can occasionally experience a bit of a weekend traffic jam, especially after a decent snowfall. Once the reservoir is safely frozen,

↙→ **Boardwalks along Little Cataraqui's wetlands and trails through its woodlands allow visitors to explore a special natural area just outside of Kingston.**

skating fans flock to the city's largest natural skating rink. A warm-up facility and an outdoor bonfire pit enhance the rink's appeal for families. Kids love the annual Maple Madness event in March, when tractor-drawn wagons take visitors to the sugar bush to learn the art of sugaring off.

During the summer months, visitors can rent kayaks and canoes, and a summer day camp operates out of the handsome Outdoor Centre, where city kids ages 6 to 11 are introduced to nature and taught outdoor skills by experienced instructors.

On spring and fall days, the quiet trails and boardwalk over the marsh are a haven for those who long to get out of the city. Wandering beside the marsh and reservoir, visitors have a great view of resident birds and small mammals scampering in the adjacent bush.

Mer Bleue Conservation Area

A taste of Ontario's post-glacial geologic history

What Makes This Hot Spot Hot?

- Mer Bleue is the second largest bog in southern Ontario.
- A boardwalk and trail network allow year-round exploration in a variety of habitats.
- The area's distinctive topography is a great way to experience eastern Ontario's geologic history first-hand.

Address: Mer Bleue Boardwalk Trail is located at the east end of Ridge Road. Other parking lots and access points to the trail networks are found elsewhere.
Tel.: N/A
Website: ncc-ccn.gc.ca/places-to-visit/greenbelt/mer-bleue

Open year-round

→ **Visitors can explore this internationally significant bog via an interpretive boardwalk.**

Ottawa is a rare city in that it boasts a bog of international significance in its midst. But Mer Bleue—which translates from French as "blue sea"—isn't just bog. This 3,500-hectare conservation area is testament to eastern Ontario's post-glacial geologic history; it also contains a mixture of wooded sand ridges, cattail marsh, old fields, wet alder and willow thickets and more.

Mer Bleue's peculiar topography stems from events that followed the end of the last ice age, when the volume of water flowing in the east-bound Ottawa River was much greater. An erstwhile channel of the river passed right over this area, stretching for more than 80 kilometres before rejoining the river's main trajectory, and two prominent and parallel sand ridges originally formed as islands within that channel. The bog itself developed later as sphagnum moss grew and peat accumulated on the poorly drained lands surrounding the ridges.

Visitors can begin by exploring the bog along a 1.2-kilometre interpretive boardwalk. Here, after passing over a cattail marsh, the ground cover below transforms into a mat of bog shrubs growing out of sphagnum moss and punctuated by billowing cotton grass. An open stand of tamarack, black spruce and birch shelters orchids, and dense spruce forest in the distance further evokes the far north. The habitat is sufficient to attract birds more typical of the boreal zone. With luck, visitors might hear sandhill cranes bugling from some distance.

Beyond the boardwalk, there are two extensive networks of walking and ski trails running on and along both sand ridges, allowing one to discover mixed forests of various ages. During spring migration, warblers such as the black-throated green warbler and mourning warbler pass through or establish their territories here. A winter jaunt on cross-country skis may reveal fisher and even moose tracks.

Presqu'ile Provincial Park

Jutting into Lake Ontario, this provincial park offers a lot of diversity in a small package

What Makes This Hot Spot Hot?

- Its unusual geography and geology create an exceptional diversity of habitats.
- It boasts some of the best migration birding on the shore of Lake Ontario.
- The park offers excellent visitor services and education programs and is conveniently located for visitors.

Address: 328 Presqu'ile Parkway, Brighton, ON K0K 1H0
Tel.: (613) 475-4324
Website: ontarioparks.com/park/presquile

Open year-round for day use; camping from May 1 to mid-October

↗ A monarch touches down at the "almost island" that is Presqu'ile.

Located roughly halfway between the Greater Toronto Area and Kingston, this provincial park is aptly named after the French word for "almost island." Presqu'ile is what is known as a tombolo—it's a gradual accretion of sand that has created a connecting spit between a limestone island and the mainland. This "almost island" projects into the smallest of the Great Lakes, and its unusual geography and geology has resulted in the park harbouring an interesting inventory of habitats.

The spit's west-facing side is exposed to the lake's wind and waves. The constant pushing action has resulted in an expansive beach, popular with swimmers, picnickers and windsurfers. The beach is framed by some of Lake Ontario's best dune habitat, which supports an incredibly diverse plant community. By contrast, the sheltered, east-facing side is home to the largest protected marsh on the northern shore of the lake, which provides habitat for abundant waterfowl,

fish and other wildlife. The "island" portion of the park is made up of mixed forests and meadows and hosts yet another community of species.

While Presqu'ile teems with life in all seasons, its spring and fall bird migrations are exceptional, and that's largely due to its varied habitats. The forests and meadows attract songbirds of every colour, while waterfowl settle in the marsh and shorebirds forage on the beach. Over 330 bird species have been recorded here, making it one of Ontario's premier migration birding locations. In autumn, monarch butterflies also rest here in large numbers before setting off across the lake.

Presqu'ile offers both camping and day-use opportunities and is equally rewarding as a day on the beach or a hike in the forest. Two visitors centres are open throughout the summer season, and education programs and guided hikes are offered daily. With so much to see, you're sure to be planning your next visit before you leave.

↑ **A boardwalk snakes through the park's grassy wetland.**

Rock Dunder

Summit this mammoth pink granite rock to view the historic Rideau Waterway

What Makes This Hot Spot Hot?

- Rock Dunder offers a panoramic view of the Rideau Waterway.
- This pink granite is a piece of ancient geologic history.
- The surrounding area is an example of Rideau country's rich biodiversity.

Address: Stanley Lash Lane off Hwy 15, just south of Morton
Tel.: N/A
Website: frontenacarchbiosphere.ca/explore/fab-trails/hike/hiking-trails/rock-dunder

Open mid-May to mid-November

↗ **A close-up of the leaves of a basswood tree, a southern delegate at home in this northern setting.**

Once the site of a wilderness camp for Boy Scouts, Rock Dunder speaks to the young adventurer in all of us. Indeed, generations of eastern Ontarians hold dear their memories of hiking the trails in this 93-hectare wilderness area, where the crux of the outing is climbing to the top of the 84-metre pink granite formation that defines Rock Dunder. Thanks to the Rideau Waterway Land Trust, which purchased the property in 2006, the experience is one that future generations will be able to cherish as well.

But Rock Dunder is also about North America's ancient origins. When sliding continental plates collided over a billion years ago, the Grenville Mountains erupted from the Earth's crumpled crust. The heat and pressure generated by the collision led to the injection of molten igneous rock into sedimentary rock deep in the roots of the range, which stretched from Canada to Mexico. Time, weather and glaciers did the rest, gradually wearing away the mountains and, in places, revealing their

inner core. Whether polished smooth or showing deep gouges and crescent-shaped chatter marks, Rock Dunder represents that core. As you gaze out from its summit upon the Rideau lakes and forests that stretch to the horizon, you are standing on the history of Earth.

At the southwest base of the rock, sheltered from the wind and warmed by the sun-drenched granite, basswood trees and other southern plants grow at the northern edge of their range. On the exposed northeast

↑ A commanding view of the Rideau Waterway awaits those who climb to the top of Rock Dunder.

end, the mosses and lichens of northern Ontario thrive.

Rock Dunder is located roughly 50 kilometres north of Kingston on Hwy 15, just south of the village of Morton. Choose from three trails: an easy 1.3-kilometre walk through mixed forest and white pines; a 2-kilometre hike to an outlook over Morton Bay; and the more challenging 3.9-kilometre loop to the summit and back.

↑ Patches of lichen such as the elegant sunburst lichen serve as bursts of colour on the granite.

Sandbanks Provincial Park

There's much, much more to this park than fun in the sun

What Makes This Hot Spot Hot?

- Sandbanks is the site of the world's largest freshwater baymouth sand barrier dune formation.
- This sandy projection into Lake Ontario makes Sandbanks a bird-migration mecca in spring and fall.
- Walking trails allow visitors to fully experience the park's dune and wetland habitats.

Address: 3004 County Road 12, RR#1, Picton, ON K0K 2T0
Tel.: (613) 393-3319
Website: ontarioparks.com/park/sandbanks

Open year-round; camping from May 1 to mid-October

One of the most popular provincial parks in Ontario, Sandbanks is located on Prince Edward County's southwestern shore. Beloved for its long stretches of stunning sand beaches and the pounding Lake Ontario surf, the park hosts large numbers of visitors who come every summer to camp, swim and bask in the sun.

Yet Sandbanks is far more than a sunny playground. Some 10,000 years ago, the wild westerly winds of Lake Ontario began to relentlessly push sand into the nooks and crannies of this headland. The vast baymouth sand barrier that eventually formed here is a dynamic, ever-changing and fragile ecosystem and is the largest freshwater sandbar and dune system in the world.

When the 1,600-hectare provincial park was first conceived in the early 1970s, it was designed to link two dune systems with the farmland and wooded area that separates them. As a result, the park protects a range of habitats that hosts

uncommon flora and fauna, and naturalists are drawn to the park in great numbers. Sandbanks is particularly valued as a birding destination during the spring and fall migrations, and more than 240 species have been observed here, including the red-headed woodpecker, pileated woodpecker, Baltimore oriole and ruby-crowned kinglet.

The park takes seriously its role in educating the public about the value of this distinctive place. In addition to daily interpretive programming during the summer, there is a 2.5-kilometre trail loop through the fragile dune and wetland habitat. Regionally rare bird species, including the marsh wren, make their home in the park. Here, too, grow distinctive dune species, such as bluet, butterfly weed and sand surge. Cyclists and hikers can take a trail through old farm pastures and hardwood woodlots, while a 12-stop interpretive trail follows the shores of the Outlet River and features two lookouts with scenic views of the marsh.

←↑ **Vegetation creeps into the park's sand dune system, while its vast sandy beaches draw sun lovers from near and far.**

Shaw Woods

A rare example of old-growth forest between Algonquin Park and Ottawa

What Makes This Hot Spot Hot?

- You'll encounter a rare vestige of virgin forest in eastern Ontario.
- The Dore Scarp, a break in the Ottawa-Bonnechere Graben runs through the Shaw Woods.
- Take a walk through the remains of abandoned homesteads that are reverting to forest.

Address: 2065 Bulger Road, North Algona Wilberforce Township, ON
Tel.: N/A
Website: shawwoods.ca

Open year-round

↗ Look closely at the forest floor to spy a giant millipede, one of the members of the vibrant invertebrate community at Shaw Woods.

A casual drive through eastern Ontario might suggest that nothing remains of the imposing primeval forests described in popular settler stories. However, Shaw Woods—acquired by the pioneering Shaw family in 1847—offers an inspiring correction to that impression. Among other features, this off-the-beaten-track gem preserves 50 hectares of old-growth forest that have never been harvested for timber, and a visit is a rare opportunity to experience first-hand the region's original forests. In addition to the old-growth stand, Shaw Woods also protects 160 hectares of wetlands and younger mixed forest over a variety of terrain, contains botanical displays, and features an Outdoor Education Centre.

From a trail network totalling 14 kilometres, visitors can enjoy three different trails. Given the rarity of the habitat, the well-maintained Old Growth Trail in the West Side trail network should be first priority for visitors with limited time. The 1.6-kilometre walk begins at the main parking lot and gradually leads up a hill stocked with very large, old hemlock, maple, birch and beech, as well as the conspicuously common basswood. The forest interior is refreshingly cool and damp and, together with the ample accumulation of humus on the forest floor, promotes a vibrant

invertebrate community underfoot that is also worth noticing, including the American giant millipede, which can be surprisingly conspicuous.

The East Side trails and the Connaught Trail allow hikers to appreciate very different habitats, including the Dore Scarp, a break in the Ottawa-Bonnechere Graben, whose formation essentially created the Ottawa Valley.

Compared with the West Side, the East Side soils may be relatively thin and the vegetation they support thereby less vigorous. Interpretive guide booklets and maps downloaded from shawwoods. ca can assist you to better appreciate the natural environments and the human influence in the Ottawa Valley.

↑ A pair of bald eagles sits atop their massive nest, which undergoes annual additions and repairs.

↖ The rugged bark of a yellow birch, a mature resident of this old-growth forest.

Stoco Fen Provincial Nature Reserve

When alkaline and acidic growing conditions exist side by side, diversity erupts

What Makes This Hot Spot Hot?

- In this unusual environment, acidic and alkaline growing conditions exist in close proximity.
- A number of provincially and regionally rare plant species can be found at the fen.
- Uncommon species of butterflies and turtles can be seen.

Address: 16151 Hwy 41, Cloyne, ON K0H 1K0
Tel.: (613) 336-2228
Website: ontarioparks.com/park/stocofen

For optimum wildflower viewing, visit during spring and summer

🚶 🔭

↗ **The carnivorous pitcher plant, which prefers acidic soil, is found at the Stoco Fen.**

Exploring Ontario's natural spaces can often be a wild and challenging ride, but every now and then, places of subtle beauty yet intense diversity show themselves. We have the fieldwork of dedicated biologists and naturalists to thank for the discovery and preservation of many of these sites. The Stoco Fen, a remarkable wetland complex located just outside the village of Tweed, can certainly be considered among their number.

A few kilometres east of Stoco Lake, the 400-hectare wetland covers a shallow depression between the limestone plateaus at the head of a valley that served as a glacial meltwater channel. Much of the wetland vegetation consists of mixed swamp forest, with cedar swamp predominating, while an open fen complex in the eastern section covers roughly 50 hectares. A mosaic of sedge meadow, shrub thickets, marl-bottomed

Clockwise from top left: The elfin skimmer, North America's smallest dragonfly; and the alkaline-soil-loving small white lady's slipper, rose pogonia and sticky false asphodel.

pools and patches of stunted cedar and larch trees, the fen has a high plant-species diversity and provides habitat for a number of provincially and regionally rare plants, the majority of which require relatively open, sunny habitats.

The most significant is a population of small white lady's slipper, an orchid that is endangered in Ontario, and Ram's head lady's slipper. Also seen here are the marsh valerian, the rose pogonia and the sticky false asphodel, a modest lily that is rare in eastern Ontario. Another denizen of alkaline environments such as the fen is a species of spikesedge known as beaked spikerush. Interestingly, while water drains into the low-lying fen from the surrounding limestone uplands, creating alkaline conditions in the sloughs, the fen's pockets of forested hummocks produce acidic-growing conditions in close proximity, an optimum environment for the carnivorous pitcher plant and sundew that flourish here.

As for wildlife, the fen is home to a number of dragonfly species, including North America's tiniest dragonfly, the elfin skimmer. The spotted turtle, one of Ontario's smallest turtles, can also be found here. At the Stoco Fen, small is beautiful.

Westmeath Provincial Park

A cherished secret among serious nature lovers

What Makes This Hot Spot Hot?

- This little-known provincial park is a hotbed of biodiversity.
- The park has extensive areas of silver maple swamp that depend on the seasonal flooding of the Ottawa River.
- Westmeath is an important natural study area thanks to its wide variety of wetland plant communities.

Address: On Bellows Bay, Lower Allumette Lake, 25 kilometres east of Pembroke
Tel.: (613) 757-2103
Website: ontarioparks. com/park/westmeath

Open year-round

The summer playground that is Sandbanks Provincial Park does double duty as the largest freshwater sandbar and dune system in the world, but a lesser star shines its own bright light a few hundred kilometres north. Westmeath Provincial Park, just east of Pembroke, was established exclusively to protect the pristine sand dune and inland wetland complexes on the south shore of the Ottawa River— remnants of the ancient Champlain Sea shoreline.

Designated a Natural Environment Park, which means only low-impact activities like hiking and swimming are allowed, 610-hectare Westmeath is unmanaged and without facilities. That's all to the good from the perspective of those who frequent this richly diverse natural area for study and recreation. Home to 300 plant species and a range of habitats, Westmeath is a favourite destination for botanists and birdwatchers.

The park's main trail passes through an open field, where dragonflies and butterflies zip around in numbers during the summer, then on to low mixed forest that shelters such birds as the brown creeper, yellow-bellied sapsucker, least flycatcher and ruffed grouse. Near a silver maple swamp, an osprey might swoop down to its nest. Along the river, you might see a spiny softshell or map turtle relaxing in the sun, or, during fall migration, spot the elusive Nelson's sparrow.

↑ The Halloween pennant dragonfly patrols the meadows at Westmeath.

⤷→ A woodland grows along a waterway running through the park, while the sandy beach along the Ottawa River is a remnant of an ancient shoreline.

← Still a hard bird to spot, the Nelson's sparrow has made a bit of a comeback at Westmeath and may be found along the river during fall migration.

A forested peninsula forms the northern end of the park and encloses the wetlands and a body of open water named Bellows Bay, a spring and fall staging area for waterfowl and shorebirds. There have been sightings here of a trumpeter swan and a Eurasian wigeon, and lesser and greater scaup, as well as redhead, northern shoveler and ring-necked ducks, have all made an appearance. A road loops around the peninsula, and you can follow the north shore of the bay and find several paths that will take you to the Ottawa River, where a refreshing summer swim on a peaceful sandy shore might be appealing after a steamy walk through the park.

Central Ontario North

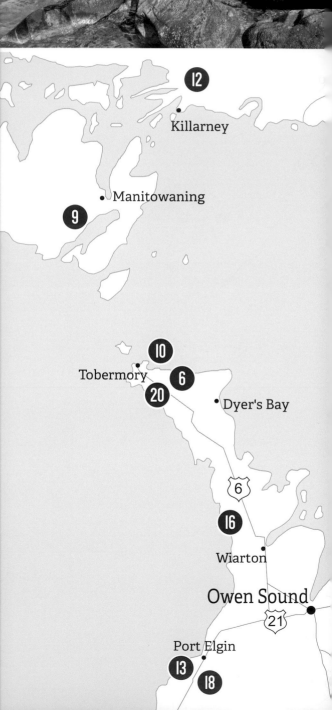

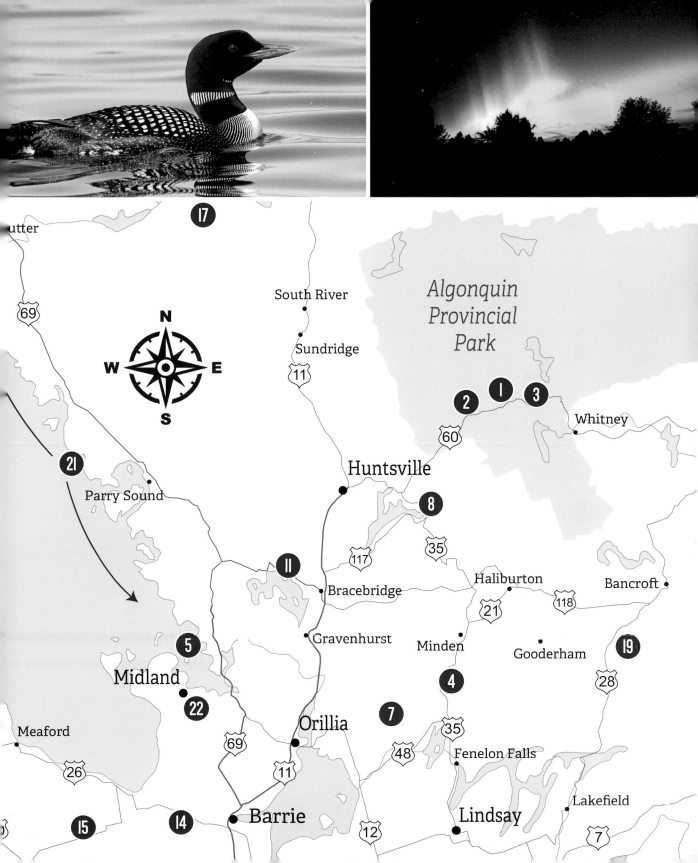

Algonquin Provincial Park's Bat Lake

A special lake with special inhabitants

What Makes This Hot Spot Hot?

- It's an acidic, fishless lake that facilitates an abundance of some uncommon species.
- There are viewing docks that offer great perspectives on the lake.
- An annual volunteer dragonfly count in Algonquin is a great starting point for budding entomologists.

Address: Algonquin Provincial Park, Box 219, Whitney, ON K0J 2M0
Tel.: (705) 633-5572
Website: algonquinpark.on.ca

Open year-round

🚶 🔭

↗ **It's not hard to see how the amber-winged spreadwing got its name.**

E stablished in 1893 on a large parcel of wilderness land between Georgian Bay and the Ottawa River, Algonquin Provincial Park was Ontario's first provincial park. A true nature gem, Algonquin has much to offer the visiting naturalist, but one of the best things about this spot is the multitude of lakes scattered across the landscape—more than 2,400 in all. Most of these lakes are full of fish that are important members of the aquatic community—both prey and predators. But Bat Lake is different. Its water is acidic—a natural phenomenon rather than the result of human activity. Indeed, research has shown that Bat Lake has been acidic for hundreds of years, too acidic, in fact, to support fish populations of any description.

How does this affect the

life of the lake? For one thing, the absence of predatory fish means that animals able to tolerate the acidic conditions can live here in higher numbers. In the spring, spotted salamanders can breed in these waters without their tadpoles being regarded as dinner by predatory fish. Instead, they emerge safely from the water and continue life on land.

Certain dragonflies and damselflies also call Bat Lake home, helping to make the lake an insect geek's nirvana. Amber-winged spreadwings (damselflies) can be seen here in the hundreds, preferring to breed in fishless water where there's no danger of winding up in the jaws of a leaping fish. The success of Bat Lake for this purpose is readily apparent if you visit here in early July—the insects are everywhere.

The Bat Lake trail passes through forests and boggy wetlands that attract many other species of dragonflies and damselflies, including emeralds, spiketails, darners, sprites and bluets. Crimson-ringed whitefaces do well in boggy environments and are very common here as well. Dragonfly watching is an increasingly popular natural history pursuit, so grab your binoculars, net and field guide, and see what you can find.

Algonquin Provincial Park's Mizzy Lake Trail

A wildlife watcher's paradise

What Makes This Hot Spot Hot?

- An easy flat trail takes you through wonderful wildlife habitat.
- There's an opportunity for many potential animal sightings against a background of misty wetlands or stunning fall colours.
- There's an excellent chance you'll meet a gray jay.

Address: Algonquin Provincial Park, Box 219, Whitney, ON K0J 2M0
Tel.: (705) 633-5572
Website: algonquinpark.on.ca

Open year-round

🚶 🔭

↗ **Bring along a few peanuts and you'll have a friend for life at Mizzy Lake: the gray jay.**

While there are good opportunities to see animals anywhere in Algonquin Provincial Park, one of the best trails for wildlife viewing is the 11-kilometre Mizzy Lake Trail. But you don't need to hike the whole thing to experience it. Drive to the northern access point off of Arowhon Road in the early morning, and walk a popular section of the trail between Wolf Howl Pond and West Rose Lake.

This hike is one of the best places in Algonquin to see all four of the "Boreal Specialties." While these four bird species—the gray jay, black-backed woodpecker, boreal chickadee and spruce grouse—are at their southern range limit in Algonquin, the park is nonetheless a great place to find them. Or rather, in the case of the gray jay, a great place for them to find you. An extremely friendly bird, the gray jay is partial to sharing trail mix with passing hikers. If one finds you, just hold out some peanuts and stand still—one might just land on your hand.

Other animals to watch for include moose. These large deer regularly use the trail as their own personal corridor, and their tracks are usually easy to see. In the fall, you

might even hear a female performing her long, drawn-out mating call. Imagine a nasally cow with a bit of a constipation problem (really).

This area can also be a good place to watch beavers and other aquatic small mammals such as otters and muskrats. If you listen carefully in the early morning, you might hear the distant call of a pack of eastern wolves. Hooded mergansers, ring-necked ducks, wood ducks, rusty blackbirds, American pipits and many warbler species can be found during the fall migration period. If you're really lucky, a hunting northern goshawk or even a great gray owl might swoop past.

↑ **At atmospheric view from the Mizzy Lake Trail, where beavers, otters and even moose might appear.**

Algonquin Provincial Park's Spruce Bog Boardwalk

Explore a bog!

What Makes This Hot Spot Hot?

- There are extensive boardwalks for easy and accessible viewing.
- It's an opportunity to get up close and personal with bog-adapted plants.
- A copy of the park's "Spruce Bog Boardwalk" trail guide will help you learn all the boggy details.

Address: Algonquin Provincial Park, Box 219, Whitney, ON K0J 2M0
Tel.: (705) 633-5572
Website: algonquinpark.on.ca

Open year-round

On this short bog trail, it's possible to really get to know one of the natural world's most interesting habitats. The Spruce Bog Boardwalk trail in Algonquin Provincial Park is a 1.5-kilometre-long loop with very little change in elevation, so all levels of hikers can comfortably explore this ancient ecosystem.

A bog is really a lake that has over hundreds of years filled in with floating mats of vegetation. As this sphagnum moss and sedge-filled vegetation dies and sinks, it becomes the peat for which bogs are largely known. The accumulated peat grows thicker and thicker, until it eventually reaches the surface of the water. At that stage, it is able to support the black spruce, the primary tree of northern boggy areas.

While the acidity of a bog doesn't allow many species of plants to survive, those that do are everywhere. Sphagnum moss serves as the base for woody shrubs such as leatherleaf and Labrador tea, with sweet gale and speckled alder also appearing closer to the creek's flowing water. All of these plants have evolved to handle the nutrient-poor conditions of the bog. The acquisition of certain nutrients is the challenge of all life, and that quest can precipitate some strange relationships. For example, many small mammals use the boardwalk

The spruce grouse makes its diet of nutrient-poor spruce needles work by eating them in great numbers.

→ **A look at one of nature's most interesting habitats.**

as a road system, and as they travel, they may leave behind some of their nutrient-rich scat. It isn't uncommon to see butterflies such as white admirals and commas sitting on the poo and probing it with their curved proboscises. Don't let this shatter your positive view of flower-visiting butterflies; these insects are tough, and many species have adapted to utilize what is available.

Speaking of strange nutrient choices, keep your eyes peeled for this spot's most sought-after resident: the spruce grouse. This boreal bird has adapted to the unthinkable in culinary menus: spruce needles. The grouse appears to survive the winter on this nutrient-poor diet by eating it in extra-large volumes. On the positive side of this menu choice, there's no risk of this bird running out of its food source in the spruce-dominated Algonquin bogs.

Altberg Wildlife Sanctuary Nature Reserve

In this protected space, two ecosystems are better than one

What Makes This Hot Spot Hot?

- The Altberg Wildlife Sanctuary is a prime example of two ecosystems living side by side.
- The reserve protects species that require a large tract of contiguous natural cover to thrive.
- Lady's slipper orchids, wild columbine and northern beech fern are among the many intriguing plants found at Altberg. There is also a wide selection of fungi.

Address: 4164 Monck Road, Kawartha Lakes, ON K0M 1K0
Tel.: N/A
Website: kawarthafieldnaturalists.org/Altberg.php

Open year-round

↗ **A creek-fed wetland in Altberg.**

It's part of what is known in Ontario as "the land between," the place where two iconic ecosystems collide. In the Altberg Wildlife Sanctuary Nature Reserve in Kawartha Lakes, the Canadian Shield and the Great Lakes-St. Lawrence Forest—the second largest forest region in the province—don't so much collide as coexist peaceably and productively. The result is a wonderfully textured landscape whose highly variable topography produces a diversity of community types. These communities, in turn, create homes for a wide-ranging number of plants and animals.

The largest nature reserve under the protection of Ontario Nature, the 471-hectare Altberg Wildlife Sanctuary is named for a former landowner who donated 110 hectares in the northern section to the Kawartha Field Naturalists (KFN) in 1983. The KFN continues to steward the nature reserve,

setting up wildlife monitoring stations, inventorying the property and making and signing trails so that the public can appreciate and enjoy this remarkable place.

Here, the Canadian Shield's rugged granite bedrock features pockets of open marsh, beaver meadow and cedar and alder swamp. The wetlands are fed by Corben Creek, which flows through the reserve and eventually empties into Four Mile Lake to the south. To the north and west, the limestone plains that characterize the Great Lakes-St. Lawrence Forest are cloaked with stands of sugar maple and ironwood interspersed with pine plantation and old fields. The woodlands create welcome habitat for a variety of birds that enjoy both the leafy overhead cover and the forest edge, including the red-shouldered hawk, hermit thrush, least flycatcher, ovenbird and a host of warblers. In the meadows, the golden-winged warbler, ruby-throated hummingbird and field sparrow can be seen going about their business. Visitors are also able to spot signs of larger mammal residents such as moose, white-tailed deer and black bears.

↑ A red-shouldered hawk on the hunt from its high perch.

↖ A moss-covered limestone outcrop in the reserve.

Beausoleil Island

Its unique geology and isolation from the mainland make Beausoleil Island Canada's reptile and amphibian hot spot

What Makes This Hot Spot Hot?

- Beausoleil is home to 33 different species of reptile and amphibian, many of which can be seen in few other places in Ontario.
- It's a rare opportunity to walk through the transition from southern mixed forests to the spectacular Canadian Shield.
- A range of camping options make this island park perfect for visitors of all experience levels.

Address: Near Port Severn, in Georgian Bay
Website: pc.gc.ca/eng/pn-np/on/georg/index.aspx

Open May 20 to October 10; check with park office for access at other times of the year

↗ **The retiring Massasauga rattler lives out of the limelight on Beausoleil Island.**

There are 63 islands in Georgian Bay Islands National Park, and eight-kilometre-long Beausoleil is the largest and most accessible. Uniquely situated on the transition zone between Ontario's southern mixed forests and the spectacular Canadian Shield, the island offers hikers a rare journey from rich, deep soils and hardwood-dominated forests in the south to the exposed granite and windswept pines in the north that are so characteristic of eastern Georgian Bay.

This unusual geological gradient provides habitat for a rich array of species. No group better illustrates the value of this "edge effect" than the reptiles and amphibians found here—there are 33 species, more than occur anywhere else in Canada. Beausoleil is a vital stronghold for these species, many of which are threatened or endangered and live in only a few other parts of Ontario. One of these is the island's most infamous inhabitant: the eastern Massasauga rattlesnake.

Beausoleil is one of the few places in Ontario that the

Massasauga still lives, and while this may put off some visitors, the fearsome reputation of this reptile is entirely undeserved. While venomous, this small snake is shy and retiring and will bite only if harassed. The opportunity to spy a Massasauga on Beausoleil is a special one, and the park works hard to promote safety, respect and appreciation for this rare animal.

As it is an island, visiting car-free Beausoleil requires a little planning. The park operates a ferry during the summer season, and several water-taxi services facilitate day-trips or camping drop-offs. There are numerous camping options, including the fully serviced Cedar Spring Campground, eight primitive campgrounds, furnished cabins and semi-permanent tent structures. Assisted camping is also available to help new campers explore this unusual piece of Canadian wilderness. A network of 12 distinct trails of varying lengths and difficulties offer visitors access to impressive views of Georgian Bay, Long Bay and the lighthouse on Brebeuf Island.

↑ A view of the Beausoleil shoreline.

Bruce Peninsula National Park

A tour of some of Ontario's most breathtaking vistas

What Makes This Hot Spot Hot?

- It features a continuous cliff with forest and lake views.
- These ancient cedars have been around since the 1300s.
- Hike the famous Bruce Trail, which ends in beautiful Tobermory.

Address: Bruce Peninsula National Park, Box 189, Tobermory, ON N0H 2R0
Tel.: (519) 596-2233
Website: pc.gc.ca/eng/pn-np/on/bruce/index.aspx

Open year-round

↗ **Cedars eke out a living in the crevices and fissures of escarpment rock.**

The Niagara Escarpment is essentially the edge of a giant basin whose centre is in the middle of the state of Michigan. Travelling north from Niagara to the eastern side of the Bruce Peninsula, the escarpment continues, though broken with watery gaps, to Manitoulin Island. From there, it runs all the way to Wisconsin's Door Peninsula, which is the western side of the Michigan Basin.

The escarpment in the Bruce Peninsula National Park is nothing short of breathtaking, and a number of park trails allow you to explore both the top and the bottom of the cliff faces. A popular destination is the Grotto, where it's possible to climb down into a partially submerged cave. Halfway Log Dump, Cave Point, Overhanging Point and Indian Head Cove are other especially appealing spots to visit.

While you may be wowed by the views alone, the trees

growing out from the sides of the cliffs will surely inspire a different sense of awe. Despite their diminutive size, some of the northern white cedars here are hundreds of years old: The oldest known specimen in the park is over 850 years old. These cedars grow very slowly due to the harsh living conditions and are part of a cliff ecosystem that includes lichens, ferns and mosses.

Wildlife and wildflower viewing in the park can easily keep a naturalist busy from early morning to nightfall. The shape of the peninsula funnels northbound spring migrant birds through the park's forests, and waterfowl can be found along the shorelines. The park has more than 30 species each of orchids and ferns as well as many other herbaceous plants waiting to be identified. A winter visit reveals the tracks of coyotes, foxes, fishers, snowshoe hares and porcupines.

↑ **The signature turquoise waters off the Bruce Peninsula.**

Carden Alvar Natural Area

A prairie habitat that thrives in Ontario

What Makes This Hot Spot Hot?

- The many rare species found in an alvar habitat make the trip a must for all budding naturalists.
- Meet the loggerhead shrike, a raptor-like songbird that impales its victims on tree thorns.
- See first-hand how the prairie smoke plant gets its name.

For directions to Carden Alvar, visit: ofo.ca/site/page/view/articles.cardenalvar **Website**: natureconservancy.ca/en/where-we-work/ontario/our-work/carden_alvar_natural_area.html

Open year-round

↗ A close-up of Carden Alvar's favourite prairie plant, the prairie smoke.

→ A wildflower meadow in the alvar attracts countless butterflies, dragonflies and damselflies.

→→ The loggerhead shrike prefers an open habitat like that found at Carden Alvar.

It's hard to say which group of naturalists loves Carden Alvar best—birders, botanists or entomologists. When you visit this globally threatened habitat, located northeast of Lake Simcoe, just be sure you're ready to look at everything this amazing place has to offer.

Due to the mostly limestone bedrock that characterizes this alvar, the thin soil at Carden Alvar stays very wet during the rainy seasons but quickly dries out when the sun shines, so only certain hardy plants are able to survive here. Thanks to a dedicated group of conservation organizations, more than 3,000 hectares have been protected.

Many familiar prairie plants have made their home at Carden Alvar, including the little blue stem, Indian paintbrush and northern dropseed, but without question, the favourite is the prairie smoke. The seed heads of this wildflower bear an uncanny resemblance to the "Truffula Trees" that appear in every naturalist's favourite story, Dr. Seuss's *The Lorax*. When a field of prairie smoke is covered in seed heads, a low mist or a wispy layer of smoke appears to hang over the field, hence the plant's name.

Because it supports a wide variety of bird species such as the sedge wren, yellow rail, common nighthawk, upland sandpiper and golden-winged warbler, in 1998, Carden Alvar was named a nationally significant Important Bird Area. The most sought-after bird here, however, is the loggerhead shrike. Endangered in Ontario, Carden Alvar represents one of their last real hopes of surviving in this province.

Carden is renowned for its many species of butterfly, dragonfly and damselfly—the Olympia marble, bronze copper, Baltimore crescent, eastern red damsel, harlequin darner, horned clubtail and Halloween pennant are all found here. With appealing names like these, how can you resist the impulse to come and see them for yourself?

Dorset Lookout Tower

A lofty view one of the greatest shows on Earth

What Makes This Hot Spot Hot?

- Climb sturdy steps to reach the top of the tower and gaze at over 800 square kilometres of autumn's colourful palette.
- There's a 2.3-kilometre trail in the surrounding forest for exploring at ground level.
- Residents can share the glory of this beautiful province with visitors from afar.

Address: 1191 Dorset Scenic Tower Rd. (just off Hwy 35)
Tel.: (705) 766-1032
Website: algonquinhighlands.ca

Open Victoria Day to Thanksgiving, 9 a.m. to 6 p.m. After Thanksgiving, the tower remains open as weather permits.

↗ **The brilliant colours of the sugar maple in autumn.**

Ontarians enjoy their share of native natural-wonder icons—the loon, freshwater lakes and rivers and pristine wilderness among them. But worldwide, the province may be best known for its fall colours. While some residents may take this spectacular seasonal display for granted, to out-of-province visitors, it's a big deal. And why not? How magical is it that the leaves of our deciduous trees suddenly change from monochromatic greens to a riot of colour before they fall to the ground?

As they prepare for winter during the fall, deciduous trees extract nutrients and chemicals from their leaves, causing the green chlorophyll to eventually break down. Combinations of previously hidden pigments and new ones that are produced in the autumn result in the fiery reds, oranges and yellows of the maples, the brilliant purples

and golds of the ashes and the reds and browns of the oaks. These contrast with the remaining green conifers for a show like no other on Earth.

As it happens, one of the best places to see this colour change is from the Dorset Lookout Tower. In 1922, a 25-metre fire tower was built just outside the village, which is located on the border of Muskoka and Haliburton counties. By the 1960s, that tower was one of more than 300 fire lookouts in Ontario. When the airplane eventually took over the job of patrolling the area for fires, however, the duties of the watchman were retired. But in 1967, Dorset's original fire tower was replaced with the 30-metre model that still stands here today, situated an impressive 142 metres above the Lake of Bays. These days, the only flames detected from the lookout are the burning colours of deciduous trees as far as the eye can see.

↑ **From the tower, visitors look out over more than 800 square kilometres.**

Flowerpot Island

Sea stack spectacular!

What Makes This Hot Spot Hot?

- The island is a geological formation hot spot with sea stacks, caves, escarpment cliffs and marl beds.
- Hike to the Flowerpot Lightstation, meet the volunteer lighthouse keeper, and enjoy the view.
- Visitors can search for unusual orchids, ferns and other plants on the loop trail.

Address: Fathom Five National Marine Park, P.O. Box 189, Tobermory, ON N0H 2R0
Tel.: (519) 596-2233
Website: pc.gc.ca/amnc-nmca/on/fathomfive/index.aspx

Open May to October

🚶 🔭 🚣 🏊 ⛺

↗ **The delicate-looking but hardy maidenhair spleenwort is one of many ferns that grow on the island.**

Once a section of a land bridge that linked the Bruce Peninsula to Manitoulin Island, Flowerpot Island is located in Fathom Five National Marine Park. In 1987, Fathom Five became Canada's first national marine park. Its 112-square-kilometre area encompasses 20 islands and the sites of 22 shipwrecks, victims of the mighty waters of Lake Huron's tumultuous Georgian Bay.

Hopping onto one of the tour ferries in Tobermory is the best way to begin your exploration of Flowerpot Island. On the trip over, you'll have a chance to see some of the local shipwrecks and learn about the tragic outcomes of the Great Lakes' unpredictable weather. Once you near the dock and the rock formations come into view, it is instantly clear how Flowerpot Island got its name. These sizable flowerpots, or "sea stacks"—one is 12 metres tall, the other is 7 metres—were formed by wave action

when the lake levels were higher than they are today.

As you wander around the island, be sure to stay on the marked trails to avoid trampling the many species of plants found here. Orchid watching is a popular pastime anywhere on the Bruce Peninsula, and here on the island, you may spy one of Ontario's most beautiful specimens, the calypso. Ferns are also bountiful, and a search of the cliff faces along the trails should reveal the delicate maidenhair spleenwort with its small leaflets and dark leaf stalks.

A large population of northern water snakes inhabits Flowerpot Island. The snakes have light-coloured bodies covered in dark patches that are especially noticeable on individuals who have just shed their skins. Older snakes often lose this pattern and are a solid grey; watch for these big snakes among the shoreline rocks near the dock on sunny days.

↑ **The flowerpot-shaped sea stack for which this island is named.**

Gordon's Park Dark Sky Preserve

The largest freshwater island in the world has a secret weapon

What Makes This Hot Spot Hot?

- Gordon's Park has nearly perfectly dark skies.
- It hosts the coolest star parties in Canada.
- With wildflowers, birds and forests, the site is a natural wonderland.

Address: 18777 Hwy 6, Tehkummah, Manitoulin Island, ON P0P 2C0
Tel.: (705) 859-2470
Website: gordonspark.com

Open May to October

Manitoulin Island lives large. For starters, it's the biggest freshwater island in the world. Part rugged northern landscape, part rolling meadow, Manitoulin is studded with rivers and more than 100 inland lakes with islands of their own. The Niagara Escarpment shows up here as well—in some places, as sheer cliffs looming more than 50 metres above the forest far below. Intriguingly, it is also home to what *SkyNews* magazine describes as "possibly the darkest reasonably accessible astronomy site in Ontario."

Located on Manitoulin's southeast corner, Gordon's Park was designated a Dark Sky Preserve in 2008 by The Royal Astronomical Society of Canada. Far from big- or even small-city lights and the telltale light domes that can appear on the horizon at some dark sky sites, the park offers stargazers a 360-degree view of almost completely black skies. It's a little bit of heaven on Earth for urban astronomers who have been battling decades of growing light pollution. A 15-minute drive from the MS *Chi-Cheemaun* ferry dock, the privately run park features eco-friendly camping on large, secluded

↑ **The northern lights dance on the Manitoulin Island horizon.**

← **The Milky Way from the dark sky reserve.**

wooded sites and hosts special events that cater to night-sky lovers throughout the season.

But there's more to Gordon's than a dark night sky. The park sits on the edge of an ancient fossil reef, and fossil hunters can see 450-million-year-old examples of giant water scorpions, brachiopods and crinoids. Nature trails through the hardwood forest wind past a pond, swamp and meadows, where wildflowers and songbirds abound in spring and summer. There's also a natural butterfly habitat, and a hike up the escarpment might lead to a glimpse of a fox in the forest shadows or a hawk soaring overhead.

↑ **The Indian paintbrush and the yellow lady's slipper nestle together at the forest edge.**

Huckleberry Rock Lookout

A spectacular view from some of the oldest rocks on Earth

What Makes This Hot Spot Hot?

- It's a relatively easy hike to stand on some of the oldest rocks on Earth.
- The spectacular view provides inarguable proof that Muskoka is one of our greatest treasures.
- The plant species growing on and around Huckleberry Rock are an excellent reminder of the rugged resilience required of life in the north.

Address: 1057 Milford Bay Road, Milford Bay, ON P1L 1X4
Tel.: (705) 765-3156
Website: ontariotrails.on.ca/trails/view/huckleberry-rock-lookout-trail

Open year-round

↗ **A fallen log becomes home for a community of fungi and lichen.**

It may sometimes seem that the Muskoka Lakes have been overtaken by monster cottages, but passionate and loyal longtime residents view this part of the province with something akin to religious fervour—for good reason. The entire region is studded with beautiful deep blue lakes and rivers carved by the glaciers of the last ice age. Located in the transition area between the northern boreal forest and the deciduous forests in the south, these lakes and rivers are flanked with deep swaths of hardwood forest interspersed with white and red pine, spruce, tamarack and hemlock.

The region sits on the southern tip of the Canadian Shield, the massive area of exposed Precambrian igneous and metamorphic rocks that covers over half of Canada and forms the backbone of North America. What better place to view the glory that is Muskoka than from atop a billion-year-old piece of the Earth's history? For more than 100 years, area residents and visitors have been doing just that from the Huckleberry Rock Lookout, where glaciation, erosion, fire and human activities have laid bare a massive slab of ancient pink granite rock.

In 1962, the massive rock

was cut to construct Muskoka Road 118, making for a dramatic drive from Port Carling to Bracebridge. But to see the bigger picture, hike the 2.5-kilometre trail that zigzags from the parking lot at Milford Bay Road to the lookout. Along the way, note the lichens and mosses eking out a living on the rocks. The meagre soil particles trapped in crevices eventually allow grasses, juniper and even white pine seedlings to germinate. Once you reach the top, you'll enjoy what is widely regarded as one of the best views in Muskoka. Take a moment, then, to consider the even more spectacular vantage point enjoyed by the birds soaring high above.

↑ **A view of Lake Muskoka from the ancient rock.**

Killarney Provincial Park

The paddling naturalist's dream destination

What Makes This Hot Spot Hot?

- There are beautiful landscapes in every direction.
- The relatively motorboat-free waters are ideal for canoeing and kayaking.
- During an evening paddle, enjoy an intimate opportunity to observe a loon.

Address: 960 Highway #637, Killarney, ON P0M 2A0
Tel.: (705) 287-2900
Website: ontarioparks.com/park/killarney

Open year-round

Ontario is a wonderful place to explore natural areas, whether by hiking rugged trails, snow-shoeing frozen wetlands, driving country roads or just sitting in a quiet forest and letting nature come to you. But exploring by canoe or kayak presents another amazing perspective for the natural-ist, and Killarney Provincial Park is the place to do it.

Killarney is primarily a wilderness park on the north shore of Georgian Bay, and its almost 50,000 hectares offer a picturesque view no matter where you turn. On the Georgian Bay edge, you can explore the smooth pink granite shoreline. In the interior, you can marvel at the rounded white hills of the La Cloche Mountain range, dotted with mixed forests and cliff edges. And everywhere, there is clear, cobalt-blue water that makes you feel as though your boat is hovering rather than floating over the surface.

Canoeing or kayaking here affords an excellent chance to really observe Ontario's official

bird, the common loon. If you approach slowly and quietly, it's often possible to come close enough to hear the loon's quiet contact hoot or watch as it preens its dappled plumage. When the loon dives, you may briefly see it swim underwater before it disappears into the lake's depths. Don't approach a loon swimming with young or one that is clearly agitated, which is a good indication that you may be close to its shoreline nest. Stressing these birds causes them to lose valuable energy that they need to raise their families.

On land, take advantage of Killarney's many kilometres of trails for hiking and snowshoeing. The park is home to moose, deer, black bears, wolves and martens, as well as more than 100 species of breeding or nesting birds. As you wander the beautiful landscape, you'll have no trouble understanding why the Group of Seven artists were committed to convincing the Ontario government to make this a park in the first place.

←↑ Come and float on the lakes in Killarney with the common loon, Ontario's provincial bird.

MacGregor Point Provincial Park

Located on one of the most beautiful sections of Lake Huron shoreline, MacGregor Point hosts an impressive bird migration and year-round wildlife

What Makes This Hot Spot Hot?

- This is a pristine piece of Lake Huron shoreline, with a diversity of inland forests and waterways.
- There is excellent migration birding and an annual spring birding festival.
- The visitors centre, friendly staff and excellent educational programming are all part of MacGregor Point's magic.

Address: 1593 Bruce Road 33, RR#1, Port Elgin, ON NoH 2C5
Tel.: (519) 389-9056
Websites: ontarioparks.com/park/macgregorpoint
friendsofmacgregor.org

Open year-round

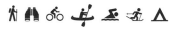

With windswept dunes and rocky beaches, the Lake Huron shoreline is like no other place in Ontario. MacGregor Point Provincial Park encompasses a seven-kilometre stretch of this unique habitat, and trails and boardwalks allow the visitor to experience it first-hand. Farther inland, the park comprises mixed forests punctuated by maple swamps, cattail marshes, bogs, fens and ponds. These varied waterways support a great diversity of wildlife.

Walking the coastal dunes often provides great viewing opportunities for a variety of bird life, including gulls, terns, shorebirds and osprey. Northern water snakes live here, too, hiding among the grasses and heading out to the lake to fish. On calmer days, dragonflies and butterflies forage along the dunes as well,

and hardy wildflowers brave the challenging environment in the spring and summer. The park's bogs support a community of carnivorous plants, including pitcher plants and the diminutive sundews. Endangered spotted turtles have been seen, and the ponds play home to a wide variety of ducks and herons.

For many naturalists, MacGregor's biggest draw is its

↑ A spotted turtle pokes its head out from a grassy shoreline.

← A dragonfly is trapped by the carnivorous spatulate-leaved sundew.

spectacular bird migration. It is a fruitful stopover for birds travelling up the shore of the lake, and on a given day in the spring, the trees may be filled with colourful warblers, vireos, tanagers and orioles. The Friends of MacGregor Point Park host the annual Huron Fringe Birding Festival here, which features guided bird hikes, workshops and guest speakers.

Whether for camping or a day visit, MacGregor Point Provincial Park exposes visitors to an ecosystem seen almost nowhere else in Ontario. A quick stop at the visitors centre, with its informative exhibits and friendly staff, will get you started in your exploration.

For those wanting a more thorough introduction, the park offers many excellent education programs throughout the summer season.

↑ A boardwalk trail through the mixed forest at MacGregor Point Provincial Park.

Minesing Wetlands

A wetland powerhouse that supports sensitive flora and fauna

What Makes This Hot Spot Hot?

- There are access spots for both canoeing and/ or hiking, skiing or snowshoeing the area.
- Minesing nurtures unusual habitats that support rare species.
- It is home to a globally endangered dragonfly that is found nowhere else in Ontario.

Address: Nottawasaga Valley Conservation Authority Administration Office, 8195 8th Line, Utopia, ON L0M 1T0
Tel.: (705) 424-1479
Websites: nvca.on.ca/ recreation/ConservationAreas/ MinesingWetlands
minesingwetlands.ca

Open year-round

🚶 🔭 🛶 ⛷

↗ The rare, wetland-loving eastern prairie fringed orchid comes with a built-in landing "lip" for pollinating insects.

Located just west of Barrie, Minesing Wetlands is a huge natural area that spans roughly 6,000 hectares. The lands are managed as a partnership between the Nottawasaga Valley Conservation Authority, the Ontario Ministry of Natural Resources (OMNR), the County of Simcoe, the Nature Conservancy of Canada, the Friends of the Minesing Wetlands and private landowners—it's a true community effort. In 1996, Minesing became a Ramsar wetland complex of international importance.

Minesing Wetlands lives up to that designation by virtue of the many different kinds of wetlands that occur within its boundaries. Some are familiar wetland types, such as the marsh, swamp and wet meadow. Others are more uncommon. Minesing possesses two provincially rare wet habitats—the Buttonbush Organic Thicket Swamp and Bur Oak Mineral Deciduous Swamp. It may also be home to southern Ontario's only Hackberry Deciduous Organic Swamp as stands of this Carolinian tree grow here in unusually wet conditions. In addition, Minesing has one of southern Ontario's largest fen complexes.

These special habitats enable an abundance of organisms to flourish, including more than 500 plants species. The provincially rare marsh valerian and beaked spike-rush, for instance, are more typically found in Atlantic coast salt marshes and rarely at inland sites such

as Minesing. Lake sturgeon and the native northern brook lamprey, both Ontario special concern species, use these waterways. More than 40 butterfly and almost 50 dragonfly and damselfly species can be seen here. One of the dragonflies recently discovered is the globally endangered Hine's emerald: Its entire Ontario range is in Minesing.

Respectful visitors can access Minesing via canoe or kayak at Willow Creek and the Nottawasaga River; for those on foot, a series of hiking trails have been created in and around the wetlands. For winter visitors, there are also showshoeing and cross-country ski trails.

↑ **High springtime water in the Minesing Wetlands.**

Nottawasaga Bluffs Conservation Area

A wild hike into the Niagara Escarpment's dark interior and back

What Makes This Hot Spot Hot?

- It's a chance to explore canyons, crevices and caves that were formed by ancient seas and glacial ice sheets millions of years ago.
- The rocks are covered with mosses, ferns and lichens that are characteristic of the flora of the heavily forested escarpment.
- A day's hike takes you into the heart of the escarpment and back up top. Please note that due to the challenges of the terrain, the conservation area recommends the buddy system for hikers.

Address: 8861 Nottawasaga Sideroad 15/16, Clearview, ON L0M 1L0
Tel.: (705) 424-1479
Website: nvca.on.ca/Pages/NottawasagaBluffs.aspx

Open year-round

As the Niagara Escarpment marches north through Ontario, it transforms every terrain it encounters. In the bucolic Nottawasaga River valley, south of Collingwood, the escarpment dramatically emerges as the Nottawasaga Bluffs. Generations ago, pioneers carved out a living here by turning the trees and limestone into wages—remnants of an original homestead and a stagecoach road can still be found. Today, the 162-hectare Nottawasaga Bluffs Conservation Area offers hikers a vivid and sometimes challenging adventure that includes a network of dark, mysterious caves, woodland trails and towering bluffs. From these, you can look out over the rolling fields tamed by our forebears.

The Keyhole Side Trail follows the escarpment slope down past massive broken pieces of rock, threading its way through a split-rock

→ The hike is marked by steep, moss-lined crevices, and visitors are urged to travel with a partner and wear appropriate footwear for rough terrain.

↙ A panoramic view of the surrounding countryside awaits hikers at the top of the bluffs.

canyon with narrow fissures and openings. As the crevice grows ever skimpier, ferns and moss cloak the walls. When you reach the keyhole, you'll have to remove your backpack to squeeze through sideways or scramble over the outcrop and descend into the last crevice. The trail then ascends to the escarpment plateau and jogs out to the bluffs. Here, the view seems to go on forever and is especially stunning in autumn.

Still to come are the Best Caves, a honeycomb of 30 to 40 caves named after a local landowner. One of these is 10 metres deep and is covered in ice, even in summer. Farther on, an outcrop named Freedom Rock has been painstakingly inscribed with social justice messages. The trail then returns you to the escarpment and a leafy walk through a quiet wood. A single-track path leads back to the parking area.

Petrel Point Nature Reserve

A quiet little reserve near the base of the Bruce Peninsula reveals that even wildflowers show Nature, red in tooth and claw

What Makes This Hot Spot Hot?

- Petrel Point is an example of Great Lakes Coastal Meadow Marsh, a globally rare habitat.
- The reserve is home to 14 orchid species as well as a handful of carnivorous plants.
- There are several other fascinating natural areas nearby, including the Oliphant Fen, the Reid Point Conservation Area and the Walker Woods Conservation Area.

Address: Petrel Point Road, South Bruce Peninsula, ON N0H 1X0
Tel.: (800) 440-2366
Website: ontarionature. org/protect/habitat/ petrel_point.php

Open from spring through fall

🚶 🔭

↗ **A boardwalk winds its way through a protected section of Great Lakes Coastal Meadow Marsh at Petrel Point.**

For outdoor lovers with a special place in their hearts for nature's subtle flourishes and idiosyncrasies, the Petrel Point Nature Reserve is a perfect afternoon outing. This reserve demands close attention and respect from visitors, especially the insect kind.

Although once described as a fen—a wetland type characterized by a deep surface layer of organic material—33-hectare Petrel Point is now regarded as an excellent example of Great Lakes Coastal Meadow Marsh, a globally rare habitat. In place of a thick layer of peat at Petrel Point, a thin surface deposit of organic matter lies over a deep layer of fine sand. Slight changes in elevation across the reserve create habitats for distinct communities of plants.

As in most fragile wetland

The carnivorous bright yellow horned bladderwort and the rose-coloured pitcher plant employ distinct strategies for trapping their prey.

reserves, a boardwalk has been installed to keep potentially destructive feet away from the vulnerable plant life. Petrel Point's narrow boardwalk winds through the meadow marsh and the dense white cedar swamp surrounding it. While in the meadow marsh, take a moment to appreciate the fact that you are gazing out on a sort of killing field. Here, the reserve's carnivorous plants make their living.

Rooted in wet soil, the horned bladderwort looks innocent enough with its bright yellow flower. Yet its simple leaves feature small bladders that open suddenly when trigger hairs are disturbed, deftly sucking in its invertebrate prey. The pitcher plant sets a different lure. Its modified leaves have a deep cavity filled with digestive fluid that is used to drown unsuspecting insects drawn by colour or nectar. Meanwhile, the sundew, one of the most-distinctive-looking varieties of carnivorous plants, attracts, arrests and absorbs insects through sticky glands spread over its leaves. It's a fascinating yet deadly community.

The reserve has a more benign allure for orchid lovers, who should keep their eyes peeled for the 14 delicate species found here, including showy lady's slipper, rose pogonia, purple-fringed orchid and broad-leaved twayblade.

Restoule Provincial Park

This provincial park's low public profile translates into on-the-ground advantages for savvy nature lovers

What Makes This Hot Spot Hot?

- At the edge of Stormy Lake, a slice of Canadian Shield towers above paddlers below.
- Restoule is easily explored by foot or by canoe.
- It's a perfect park in which to find a peaceful place to sit and watch the wildlife around you.

Address: 8818 Highway 534, Restoule, ON P0H 2R0
Tel.: 705-729-2010
Website: ontarioparks.com/park/restoule

Open from early April to end of November; camping from mid-May to mid-October

↗ The long-lived snapping turtle, with its powerful jaws, is probably best avoided when out of the water.

Sandwiched between Restoule Lake and Stormy Lake southwest of North Bay, Restoule Provincial Park extends along the shores of the Restoule River. These beautiful waterways serve as an invitation to explore the area by canoe or kayak. Paddle along the base of the towering Stormy Lake Bluffs and look up, way up, for an intimate view of geologic history. In this region, roughly 550 million years ago, a huge parcel of land split and fell away along a fault line, creating a long, steep-walled depression—now filled with the waters of Stormy Lake—that is the southern edge of the Ottawa Valley Rift.

The park offers much to the avid hiker as well the paddler. There are 15 kilometres of trail through a mixed forest of red oak, yellow birch, red maple and sugar maple, but perhaps the most rewarding hike is along the seven-kilometre Fire Tower Trail. This route explores a variety of forested areas, finishing with a spectacular view of Stormy Lake from the 100-metre-tall Stormy Lake Bluffs.

Wildlife watching is an essential part of any visit to Restoule. The two lakes harbour some extremely large snapping turtles as well as river otters, while snakes and turtles live in the park's wetlands. The area is also home to one of Ontario's largest herds of white-tailed deer. The Great Lakes-St. Lawrence forest here includes rare black ash

swamps. More than 90 species of birds are found in the park, and birdwatchers especially appreciate the many species of warblers and their disparate foraging strategies. The Blackburnian warbler typically stays high in the treetops, while the black-and-white warbler scoots around on large branches and tree trunks in a style reminiscent of the nuthatch. Meanwhile, the northern waterthrush forages on the ground in wet areas. By feeding in different spots and in different ways, these like-sized birds avoid competing with one another, ensuring that there is more food for all.

↑ **A long view from the Stormy Lake Bluffs.**

Saugeen Bluffs Conservation Area

Along this mostly lazy river, you'll find a little drama and a lot of nature

What Makes This Hot Spot Hot?

- This family-friendly conservation area has 200 camping spots, picnic shelters and other amenities.
- A trail network creates easy opportunities for hiking and exploring.
- A hike to the bluffs offers a spectacular view of the river and surrounding countryside.

Address: 132 Saugeen Bluffs Road, RR#3, Paisley, ON N0G 2N0
Tel.: (519) 353-7206
Website: www.svca.on.ca/ca.php?page=saugeenbluffs

Open May to October

→ **The mostly gentle Saugeen River is a favourite of paddlers.**

From its headwaters near Dundalk, the Saugeen River flows in a downward course across this region's classically rolling countryside, carving its way through farmland as it heads to Lake Huron, near Southampton. The third largest river system in southern Ontario, the Saugeen falls a total of 353 metres over its roughly 200-kilometre length.

Paddlers have a special affection for this typically gentle river, which features occasional flurries of rapids and eddies and three dams that require short portages. Along the route, shoreline forest offers some cover from the sun, and there are lots of opportunities to appreciate the wildlife activity on the river, from a prehistoric-looking blue heron flapping overhead to beavers and muskrats ducking under the water to avoid human scrutiny. The river's watershed has been identified as an Environmentally Significant Area, and species such as Goldie's fern, Turk's cap lily and the endangered butternut tree can be found here.

The deep river valley's clay plain is dramatically showcased in the 121-hectare Saugeen Conservation Area, north of Paisley. Here, the clay bluffs rise up to 30 metres, giving visitors a glorious view of the river and the surrounding countryside. A fully developed trail system allows hikers and campers to investigate flora and fauna in a mature forest populated by hard maple, elm, beech and oak. Springs originating in the area's ravines flow to the Saugeen, creating a natural corridor that enables species movement.

Silent Lake Provincial Park

A peaceful, pristine fragment of southern Canadian Shield

What Makes This Hot Spot Hot?

- The park is a silent, scenic retreat with ample opportunities for recreation or relaxation.
- A hot spot for dragonflies, the park is home to species that are rarely seen elsewhere.
- Visitors can appreciate a great diversity of boreal wildlife and landscapes in a southern locale.

Address: 1589 Silent Lake Park Road, Bancroft, ON K0L 1C0
Tel.: (613) 339-2807
Website: ontarioparks. com/park/silentlake

Open mid-May to mid-October; check website for winter camping dates

🚶 🔭 🚴 🛶 🏊 🚣 ⛺

↗ **This dragonhunter looks armed for action.**

Head out for a paddle on Silent Lake, and it won't take long to understand where it gets its name. Far removed from cities and highways and free of noisy motorboats, the Bancroft-area provincial park is an ideal place to take some time to enjoy the peace and tranquility of nature. There are plenty of waterways and trails for paddling and hiking and lots of accessible shorelines for setting up a chair and taking it all in.

No matter how you choose to enjoy Silent Lake, there is one group of residents you will inevitably encounter: the dragonflies. These aerial hunters are denizens of the boreal forest, and Silent Lake is a mecca for them. Brilliant flashes of blue, green or yellow, they dance along the water's edge or patrol over the trails in search of the smaller insects that make up their diet. Mosquitoes and black flies are an especial favourite, so dragonflies make welcome campsite neighbours.

The keen observer may spot two large local specialities with interesting names. The Cyrano darner's moniker may seem nonsensical, until a close-up look reveals the rather generous "nose" it

shares, along with its name, with the well-known literary character. The meaning of the dragonhunter's name, on the other hand, is somewhat easier to fathom. This enormous, mostly yellow dragonfly hunts mainly its smaller relatives by coursing along the shoreline. Dragonhunters can be seen throughout the park, so watch for their powerful flight from the shore or canoe.

If dragonflies don't excite you, Silent Lake still has much to offer. The park is home to a great many mammals, birds, frogs and butterflies, as well as the spectacular rocky scenery of the Canadian Shield. The beautiful campsites range from fully serviced to walk-in, and the park is ideal for day visits too. Canoes can be rented by the hour, and two sandy beaches are perfect for a swim or picnic.

↑ **A peaceful scene from Silent Lake.**

Singing Sands Beach

Where a wildflower paradise meets family fun at the beach

What Makes This Hot Spot Hot?

- It's a botanist's dream destination with lots of interesting plant species.
- There are spectacular sunsets and wildflowers for photographers.
- The combination of beach and nature is guaranteed to make every family member happy.

Address: Dorcas Bay Road, Bruce Peninsula National Park, Tobermory, ON N0H 2R0
Tel.: (519) 596-2233
Website: pc.gc.ca/eng/pn-np/on/bruce/index.aspx

Open year-round

🚶 👓 🏊

↗ **Among the many orchids to watch for at Singing Sands is the grass pink.**

Located on the Lake Huron shoreline in Dorcas Bay, Singing Sands Beach is part of the Bruce Peninsula National Park. The beach's gradual sandy slope into the lake distinguishes it from much of park's hallmark rocky escarpment. The sheltered bay is very shallow, making it a great spot for families to enjoy some splash time. Curiously, under certain wind conditions, an effect much like that of a freshwater tide may occur, with water levels slowly creeping up and back down the sandy beach. Kids and parents with a stick and a little ingenuity can spend hours carving out their own mini river systems in the sand.

As a break from the sun and surf, a hike inland along the trails is sure to charm the whole family. Woodpeckers and warblers vie with butterflies and blooms for your attention. The forests, fens and scrub hold colourful blooming plants such as

the dwarf lake iris, Indian paintbrush, wood lily and blue-eyed grass, and kids are delighted to discover plants that actually eat insects—carnivorous wildflowers like the pitcher plant, linear-leaved sundew and butterwort.

Last, but certainly not least, are the area's orchids. One in particular has made Singing Sands a famous destination for botanists: the Ram's Head lady's slipper. This delicate beauty blooms from late May to early June and is sure to wow any nature nut. Other showy orchids to watch for are the yellow lady's slipper, rose pogonia and grass pink. And remember, if you work up a sweat on your nature walk, a refreshing dip at the beach is never far away.

↑ **Sunset on the beach.**

Thirty Thousand Islands

The world's largest freshwater archipelago

What Makes This Hot Spot Hot?

- There are impressive Canadian Shield landscapes at the water's edge.
- Georgian Bay's clear water is perfect for under-the-surface wildlife watching.
- Watch out for rare reptiles and plant life on your hikes.

Websites: ontarioparks. com; pc.gc.ca/eng/pn-np/on/ georg/index.aspx; Georgian Bay Land Trust: gblt.org/

Contact individual parks for information about seasonal closures.

↗ **The smooth green snake is arguably Ontario's prettiest snake species.**

The eastern shoreline of Georgian Bay is one of Ontario's most dramatic landscapes. Windswept, rugged and wild, it is dotted with tens of thousands of islands collectively known as the Thirty Thousand Islands. It's the world's largest freshwater archipelago, and while private cottages are plentiful, there are many government-run parks that the public is welcome to enjoy and explore—Killbear, Awenda and Sturgeon Bay provincial parks and Georgian Bay Islands National Park among them.

In addition, the Georgian Bay Land Trust and the Nature Conservancy of Canada oversee several properties that allow visitors as well. This mixture of accessible and non-accessible areas creates the best of both worlds: beautiful places for the naturalist to visit and reservoirs of wildlife habitat to protect nature from human harm.

The ideal—and sometimes only—way to explore the Thirty Thousand Islands is by watercraft. Kayaking is the preferred means for many reasons: It offers access to very

shallow water, easy manoeuvrability and a quiet approach for wildlife watching. While floating around in a kayak, you might see a muskrat or northern map turtle swim underneath you or a northern pike slowly turn its body before torpedoing forward to grab a minnow. Along the shorelines, watch for the praying mantis-like water scorpions seizing a smaller aquatic insect or a giant water bug father carrying his mate's eggs on his back.

While hiking an island's gorgeous granite formations, look out for Ontario's only lizard species, the endangered five-lined skink. Young individuals stand out with their brilliant blue tails, while the older generations are duller overall. Another colourful reptile found here is the smooth green snake, which slithers along looking very much like a live lime-green shoelace. Watch for brilliant wildflowers, too, such as Kalm's lobelia and the cardinal flower. And don't forget to finish up by appreciating the day's last colours as the shimmering sun sets across the bay.

↑ **Just one of the spectacular Thirty Thousand Islands.**

Wye Marsh Wildlife Centre

Home of the resurgent trumpeter swan, this centre offers Ontarians hands-on experience in the value of wetlands

What Makes This Hot Spot Hot?

- Wye Marsh does double duty as a classroom wetland, where you can learn about our natural heritage and our natural resources.
- It is one of the few places in Ontario where you can come face-to-face with the trumpeter swan.
- The centre supports a wildflower garden populated with indigenous plants that attract birds, bees and butterflies.

Address: 16160 Highway 12 East, Midland, ON L4R 4KR
Tel.: (705) 526-7809
Website: wyemarsh.com

Open year-round

↗ **The marsh in autumn.**

The statistics are stark. As a result of land development, agricultural runoff and invasive species, more than 70 percent of Canadian wetlands have disappeared. That's a concern for all of us, because wetlands play an integral role in how the rest of our world works. They clean and filter our fresh water, prevent shoreline erosion, decompose vegetative matter, recycle nutrients and provide habitat and breeding grounds for a wide range of wildlife. That's why the Wye Marsh Wildlife Centre has put education at the heart of its programming.

About five kilometres east of Midland, the 1,000-hectare Wye Marsh nestles along the southern shore of Georgian Bay. Designated a Provincially Significant Wetland, it comprises primarily cattail marsh, with pockets of fen, dense coniferous swamp, upland forests and shallow Wye Lake (a.k.a. Mud Lake) at its hub. Today, 64 nesting bird species, including the black tern, least bittern, Virginia rail and marsh wren, reside here. Wye

Marsh is also famously home to the largest concentration of trumpeter swans in Ontario. That's due to the dedicated work of marsh supporters and biologist Harry Lumsden, who launched a program in the 1980s to bring the trumpeter back to its traditional habitat. It had been hunted to extirpation a century before.

With 25 kilometres of groomed trails and boardwalks, visitors have access to the marsh year-round. Bikes and ski and snowshoe equipment can be rented, and rustic cabins are available for overnight group stays. Guided eco-tours by canoe, kayak and snowshoe, day and overnight camps for kids and annual festivals round out the centre's generous outreach initiatives. Visit this beautiful wetland to see environmental stewardship in action. While you're here, be sure to spend some time observing the magnificent trumpeter swan, which came so close to permanently vanishing from Ontario.

↑ **A healthy cygnet, the successful result of Wye Marsh's trumpeter swan restoration project.**

↖ **The plant life is lush in the summertime marsh.**

Northern Ontario

Nakina

Lake Nipigon

Geraldton

Beardmore

Long Lake

Hornepayne

Nipigon

Terrace Bay

Kabinakagami Lake

Marathon

White River

Pukaskwa National Park

Thunder Bay

Wawa

Lake Superior Provincial Park

Kakabeka Falls Provincial Park

Welcome to the wild Niagara of the north

What Makes This Hot Spot Hot?

- Far from wax museums and food vendors, this wilderness waterfall is impressive four seasons of the year.
- The park runs summertime programs in which visitors can learn about the area's geology and native wildlife and flora.
- The trails and viewing platforms are easily accessed and offer a variety of views.

Address: Box 252, Kakabeka Falls, ON P0T 1W0
Tel.: (807) 473-9231
Website: ontarioparks.com/park/kakabekafalls

Open year-round for day use; camping from Victoria Day weekend through Thanksgiving

↗ **A bald eagle cruises above the gorge, in search of spawning salmon.**

Just west of Thunder Bay, this five-square-kilometre park embraces the thunderous waterfall named for the Ojibwe word *gakaabikaa*, which means "waterfall over a cliff." And fall Kakabeka does, as the iron-stained Kaministiquia River plunges 40 metres into a massive gorge carved from the underlying Precambrian Shield. Below the waterfall, the river flows through an expansive floodplain created after the last ice age.

While Kakabeka Falls is just off the Trans-Canada, it has none of the commercial trappings that attach to its larger, citified southern cousin, Niagara. Apart from a visitor centre, boardwalk and viewing platforms, the park maintains an exhilarating wilderness setting. That makes it easy to imagine the wonder these powerful, churning waters must have inspired in the region's indigenous population and the voyageurs who travelled these waterways much later.

Visitors are welcome to follow the boardwalk and pedestrian bridge that wrap around the top of the falls. From here, there's a magnificent view of the river, the waterfall and the unstable shale escarpments that line the gorge below. Access to the gorge itself is prohibited because of the rock's fragility, but encased within the eroding rock are 1.6-million-year-old fossils. In the autumn, bald eagles can be seen gliding along the gorge in search of salmon swimming upriver to spawn.

There are six park trails, one of which is a 1.25-kilometre scenic loop through woods that is part of the historic

portage used by early travellers. Another features a steep hike down into the river valley and offers a look at nearby picturesque Little Falls. The four-kilometre Poplar Point Trail loop provides opportunities for wildlife spotting and birdwatching, and in fall, the golden colours of the aspen forest are striking. In winter, the trail is groomed for cross-country skiing.

A true northern Ontario wonder, Kakabeka Falls won't be anybody's second greatest disappointment.

↑ **The explosive Kakabeka Falls.**

← **A park boardwalk passes through a corridor of conifers.**

Lake Superior Provincial Park

The shoreline of this wilderness park tells a haunting tale of human and geological history

What Makes This Hot Spot Hot?

- The Lake Superior shoreline in the park is a visual essay on the region's geological history.
- A short rugged path from Hwy 17 takes you to one of the most visited pictograph sites in Canada, accessible on foot only when Superior is calm.
- The Trans-Canada/Hwy 17 bisects the park, which has 11 hiking trails and a wide selection of campsites.

Address: P.O. Box 267, Wawa, ON P0S 1K0
Tel.: (705) 856-2284
Website: ontarioparks. com/park/lakesuperior

Open May to mid-October

↗ **A sandy beach along the shoreline of the greatest of the Great Lakes.**

Over a billion years ago, tectonic plates shifted and fractured the continent's bedrock spine, producing a massive rift valley through the region that now includes Lake Superior. In time, volcanic and glacial activity eventually filled the rift with a sequence of rocks until, after the last ice age, meltwaters created the greatest of the Great Lakes. Visitors to the shoreline in Lake Superior Provincial Park, which sprawls 1,550 square kilometres along the northeastern coast of Superior, will find vivid evidence of the lake's tumultuous origin.

At Agawa Bay, roam one of the longest beaches on Superior's north shore, built with sand and cobble swept here by the Agawa River from inland beach terraces over thousands of years. Note the water-scoured bedrock at the southern end of the beach, forged from basalt, granite and gneiss. Across the headland's outcrops run ancient fractures filled with minerals: A dark basaltic stripe is sandwiched between

pink granite and grey gneiss;
nearby, a stripe of white granite boldly snakes through a
bed of gneiss. On a sun-soaked
summer day, it's a peaceful
scene that belies a raucous history of ruptured landscapes
and erupting molten rock.

There's a story of human history here as well. A short drive
north of Agawa Bay on the
Trans-Canada is the turnoff to
the Agawa Rock pictographs.
A trail descends through rock
chasms and massive broken
boulders to the lake, where a
rock ledge runs along the base

↑ On a calm day, paddlers are able to
access the Agawa Rock pictographs.

of a 30-metre-high vertical
cliff. Here, roughly 400 years
ago, Ojibwe recorded their
daily lives, dreams and visions
on the sheer face of this white
crystalline granite using a mix
of red ochre and clay. After
centuries of sun, wind, waves
and winter storms, these
sacred paintings endure.

↑ A centuries-old Ojibwe pictograph
on the cliff face at Agawa Rock.

Ouimet Canyon

Often called 'Canada's Grand Canyon,' Ouimet Canyon is a rare opportunity to experience a wall of rock with a sheer drop of 100 metres

What Makes This Hot Spot Hot?

- It's a rare opportunity to witness a sheer drop of 100 metres.
- The canyon features a massive rock column known as the Indian Head.
- Nearby privately owned Eagle Canyon Adventures boasts Canada's longest zipline and longest suspension footbridge.

Address: Ouimet Canyon Provincial Park, c/o Sleeping Giant Provincial Park, RR#1, Pass Lake, ON P0T 2M0
Tel.: (807) 977-2526
Website: ontarioparks.com/park/ouimetcanyon

Open May to October

↗ **Early coniferous fruit offer a burst of colour.**

There's no shortage of spectacular views for people travelling along the northern shoreline of Lake Superior, but there's unanimous agreement that a short detour leading to Ouimet Canyon is well worth taking. Less than an hour's drive northeast of Thunder Bay and about 15 kilometres off the Trans-Canada/Hwy 17, the two-kilometre-long protected canyon, part of Ouimet Canyon Provincial Park, offers a rare glimpse into the region's geological past.

The Ouimet Canyon was formed when the weight of glaciers and their meltwater split open the volcanic rock that characterizes Lake Superior's northern shore. The eroding effect of wind and rain over time has continued that work, as evidenced by the field of fallen rocks at the base of the canyon.

After a modest entrance fee and an easy hike in from the parking lot, visitors can take the measure of the

100-metre-deep, 150-metre-wide gorge from two viewing platforms that are linked by a trail and boardwalk. The view across the canyon is of a vast rock cliff face shaped by the distinctive vertical joints of volcanic rock. To the north, the canyon winds its way into the hills that envelop the area. To the south, the canyon settles into a valley and a stunning wide-angle glimpse of Lake Superior. On an overcast day, the vista can take on an almost eerie, otherworldly atmosphere.

The virtually sunless, wind-free zone that exists at the canyon's ground floor offers up yet another intriguing feature. Here, as in the garden of Oscar Wilde's *Selfish Giant*, ice and snow persist year-round, promoting the growth of vegetation that would otherwise grow only in Arctic and subarctic zones to the north. To preserve and protect this fragile plant ecosystem, visitors are not allowed to travel to the bottom of the canyon.

↑ The sheer cliffs of the Ouimet Canyon rise up from the sunless, rocky canyon floor.

Potholes Provincial Nature Reserve

A stopoff at the peaceful Kinniwabi River offers insight into the country's tempestuous geological past

What Makes This Hot Spot Hot?

- Visit a site where powerful subglacial rivers dramatically transformed the riverbed.
- In this ancient glacial valley, you'll view a miniature waterfall in the midst of the boreal forest.
- A short hike and a brief education in natural heritage are a peaceful break from a long driving trip.

Address: 190 Cherry Street, Chapleau, ON P0M 1K0
Tel.: (705) 864-3114
Website: ontarioparks.com/park/potholes

Open mid-June to early September; day use only

After you've seen the Wawa Goose, rumoured to be the most photographed landmark in North America, head about 50 kilometres west and south on Hwy 101, and stop off at Potholes Provincial Nature Reserve. Here, you'll see a captivating real-life tableau that provides yet another glimpse of the transmogrifying impact glaciers have had on the Ontario landscape.

We're officially in Algoma Country, a vast piece of real estate that consumes almost 50,000 square kilometres of true northeastern Ontario wilderness. The region is studded with inland lakes and rivers, and the boreal forest is populated by yellow birch, white spruce and balsam fir, with a mix of sugar maple and eastern white cedar. On the river terraces, white birch and black spruce grow, and

in the woodland, the songs of warblers may be heard.

But at the Kinniwabi River, the most intriguing sound is that of the surging waters swirling around the potholes left behind by the ice sheet which covered Canada between 20,000 and 10,000 years ago. As the bottom of the ice sheet melted, water poured beneath the ice. Some of these meltwaters carved

gorges into the hard bedrock; others grabbed up granite boulders that, once caught in the swirling eddies of the meltwater flow, effectively became tools that ground away at the bedrock on the river floor. Once a spot was worn, according to geologist Nick Eyles, the driving water whirled the boulder in place, where it mimicked the action of a powerful grinding tool. Eventually, the shallow depression was worn into a deep, circular, smooth-sided pothole, around which the river's waters continue to eddy and flow.

Come for the potholes, but stay for a walk along the short interpretive trail and boardwalk to appreciate the sedges and flowering plants that grow on the riverbank. Enjoy a picnic lunch before you get back on the road.

←↑ Two views of the transformed landscape created by glacial meltwaters.

Pukaskwa National Park

This park puts fresh life into the overworked descriptor 'pristine wilderness'

What Makes This Hot Spot Hot?

- It's the only national park in Ontario that is designated a wilderness park.
- A trip to Pukaskwa is for the fit and self-reliant nature lover.
- You'll experience the raw beauty of Ontario's natural world at its best.

Address: Highway 627, Heron Bay, ON P0T 1R0
Tel.: (807) 229-0801
Website: pc.gc.ca/eng/pn-np/on/pukaskwa/index.aspx

Open year-round; campgrounds are open from spring to fall

→ **The clean, cold waters of Superior sweep into shore at Pukaskwa.**

You can reach Ontario's only wilderness national park by the most conventional of routes. Simply turn off the Trans-Canada onto Hwy 627, which drops you at the Hattie Cove Campground. Once you exit your vehicle and look around, you'll quickly realize you've left civilization far behind.

Pukaskwa National Park sprawls across 1,878 square kilometres of some of the province's most dynamic landscape. It's the very definition of "Shield Country." On its western edge, Pukaskwa hugs the dramatic undulations of the Lake Superior shoreline, where massive headlands push into the waters of Canada's tempestuous inland sea, creating a dazzling series of deep, sculpted bays. Punctuating the coast are beaches of white sand and water-smoothed stone and stretches strewn with massive pieces of timber tossed ashore by the tumultuous Superior waves.

Inland is a world of rock-lined lakes, surging rivers and intact boreal forest that serves as a natural habitat for northern wildlife, such as moose, black bears and wolves. A small, elusive herd of woodland caribou also makes its home here, though the forest industry operating in adjacent lands threatens its territory.

The intrepid might consider exploring Pukaskwa by water, but be forewarned: The typically cold and unpredictable Lake Superior waters and winds will inevitably pin down paddlers for days at a time. For hikers, there are moderate trails that lead to some of the park's best vantage points. The Beach Trail winds through North, Middle and Horseshoe Beaches; the Southern Headland Trail leads to the lakeside, where, on a late-summer afternoon, you might relax on the sun-warmed granite to the sounds of Superior lapping against the shore. The more ambitious can undertake the 18-kilometre return hike to the White River Suspension Bridge, which soars 23 metres over Chigamiwinigum Falls.

Sleeping Giant Provincial Park

An iconic silhouette on Lake Superior anchors one of Ontario's most unforgettable parks

What Makes This Hot Spot Hot?

- The park offers some of northwestern Ontario's most spectacular views of Lake Superior.
- An elaborate trail system allows visitors a variety of routes by which to explore the park.
- Cross-country skiing and snowshoes are perfect ways to experience the northern winter.

Address: Pass Lake, ON P0T 2M0
Tel.: (807) 977-2526
Website: ontarioparks. com/park/sleepinggiant

Open year-round

↗ **The Giant in majestic profile.**

Not many Canadian cities boast a view like the one from Thunder Bay's harbour, which captivates residents and visitors alike. They may be looking at Lake Superior's Sibley Peninsula, but what mesmerizes them is a massive formation of mesas and sills that resembles nothing so much as a super-sized human stretched out on his back. Since 1944, the home of this serene, majestic figure has been known as

Sleeping Giant Provincial Park, a fitting tribute to a legendary icon that has so vividly captured the imaginations of all who gaze upon him.

Fifty-two kilometres long and 10 kilometres wide, the peninsula is almost entirely occupied by the park. The western half is dominated by highlands that rise some 380 metres above the surface of the largest, deepest Great Lake; the gentler eastern lowlands reach 75 metres. The

Sleeping Giant has the longest trail system of any Ontario Park—more than 100 kilometres—from which hikers can explore Lake Superior's classically rugged shoreline, with its towering cliffs, breathtaking vistas, beaches and coves. Paddlers will enjoy the crystal-clear waters as they investigate the park from the water.

Dense boreal forest, inland lakes and an elaborate coastline create perfect habitat for a wide selection of songbirds, raptors, shorebirds and waterfowl. Of the more than 200 bird species recorded in the park, roughly 75 nest here. At the tip of the peninsula, adjacent to the park, is the Thunder Cape Bird Observatory.

↑ A favourite hiking destination in the park is the Sea Lion, a feature of the area's geological history and the relentless wave action of Superior.

For those looking for four-legged wildlife, a variety of mammals, including bears, foxes, deer and hares, may appear along trails and roads.

The serious nature lover can reserve one of the 40 back-country campsites at Sleeping Giant; there are also 200 camp-sites for tents and recreational vehicles. Given the sheer scope of the park, visitors may not be satisfied with a simple day visit. And once you are here, the Ojibwe legends that surround the Sleeping Giant may very well compel you to linger.

↑ The easiest of the *Empidonax* flycatchers to identify, thanks to its yellow underparts, the yellow-bellied flycatcher is considered a bird of the boreal forests and bogs.

Index

Photo Credits

Front cover: Flowerpot Island © shipfactory/Shutterstock. Inset photographs from left: moose © Oliver S/Shutterstock; cardinal © Steven Russell Smith Photos/Shutterstock; monarch butterfly © Kyle Horner; yellow lady's slipper © Chris Earley.

Back cover, top: Sandbanks Provincial Park © marevos imaging/Shutterstock; middle: Tommy Thompson Park © Hartley Millson; bottom: Wye Marsh Wildlife Centre © Ryan Adams.

13 top and bottom © Chris Earley; 14 © Brian Lasenby/Shutterstock; 15 © Paul Reeves Photography/Shutterstock; 16 © Ed Schneider/Shutterstock; 17 © Simon Wilson/Nature Conservancy of Canada; 18 © Brian Lasenby/Shutterstock; 19 © Daniel Holm/The Word & Image Studio courtesy Ausable Bayfield Conservation Authority; 20 © Chris Earley; 21 top and bottom © Essex Region Conservation Authority; 22 © Paul Sparks/Shutterstock; 23 © Hamilton Conservation Authority; 24 © Lois McNaught; 25 clockwise from top: © Essex Region Conservation Authority, © Kyle Horner, © Chris Earley; 26 © Alan Watson; 27 © Al Standring/Grand River Conservation Authority; 28 © Hamilton Conservation Authority; 29 © Hamilton Conservation Authority; 30 © Candice Talbot; 31 top and bottom © rck_953/Shutterstock; 33 top © Kim Broadbent; 33 bottom © Ivan Kuzmin/Shutterstock; 34 © Chris Earley; 35 top © Essex Region Conservation Authority; 35 bottom © Chris Earley; 36 © Jennifer Howard/Trumpeter Swan Coalition; 37 © Gary Lane/Trumpeter Swan Coalition; 38 © Chris Earley; 39 top © SF photo/Shutterstock; 39 bottom © Chris Earley; 40 © Chris Earley; 41 © Thames Talbot Land Trust/Nature Conservancy of Canada; 43 clockwise from top © Candice Talbot; © Peter Schwarz/Shutterstock; © Candice Talbot; 44 © Paul Tessier/Shutterstock; 45 © robert cicchetti/Shutterstock; 47 top © Tom Preney/Ojibway Nature Centre; 47 bottom © Kyle Horner; 48 © Ross Wilson/Ausable Bayfield Conservation Authority; 49 © John Jimmo/Ausable Bayfield Conservation Authority; 50 © Psychotic Nature/Shutterstock; 51 © Jukka Palm/Shutterstock; 52 © Brian Lasenby/Shutterstock; 53 © Elena Elisseeva/Shutterstock; 54 © Kevin Wells Photography/Shutterstock; 55 © Chris Hill/Shutterstock 56 © Ausable Bayfield Conservation Authority; 57 © Daniel Holm/The Word & Image Studio courtesy Ausable Bayfield Conservation Authority; 58 © Gregory Synstelien/Shutterstock; 59 top and bottom © Ian MacDonald; 60 © Ed Schneider/Shutterstock; 61 © Alan Watson; 62 © Tys Theysmeyer/Royal Botanical Gardens; 63 top © Tys Theysmeyer/ Royal Botanical Gardens; 63 bottom © Chris Earley; 64 © Dennis W. Donohue/Shutterstock; 65 © Sharon Drummond; 66 © Chris Earley; 67 top © Neil Hardwick/Shutterstock; 67 bottom © Chris Earley; 68 © Ryan M. Bolton/Shutterstock; 69 © Chris Earley; 70 © Tony Campbell/Shutterstock; 71 top © Ontario Parks; 71 bottom © Kenneth Keifer/Shutterstock; 72 clockwise from left © PhotoSerg/Shutterstock; © Hartley Millson; © Bruce MacQueen/Shutterstock; © Nature Conservancy of Canada; 74 © Chris Earley; 75 © Maria Papoulias; 77 © Ian C. Whitworth Photography; 78 © Kyle Horner; 79 © Jeff Feverston/Shutterstock; 80, 81 all photos © Nature Conservancy of Canada; 83 © Teri Virbickis/Shutterstock; 84 © Chris Earley; 85 © Kelly Balkom; 86 © Credit Valley Conservation; 87 © Credit Valley Conservation; 88, 89 all photos © Hartley Millson; 90 © PhotoSerg/Shutterstock; 91 © PhotoSerg/Shutterstock; 92 © DMS Foto/Shutterstock; 93 © Friends of Seaton Trail; 94 © Bruce MacQueen/Shutterstock; 95 © Chris Earley; 96 © Paul Tessier/Ontario Nature; 97 © Craig Sterken/Shutterstock; 98 © Kyle Horner; 99 © Hartley Millson; 100 © Paul Zammit/Toronto Botanical Garden; 101 © Maddie Maillet/Toronto Botanical Garden; 102 clockwise from left © Owen Bjorgan, © Owen Bjorgan, © Feng Yu/Shutterstock, © Owen Bjorgan, © Christopher Gardiner/Shutterstock; 105 © R.G. Rutkay; 106 © Peter Schwarz/Shutterstock; 107 clockwise from top © K. Smith/Niagara Conservation Authority, © Terry Carter/Ontario Ministry of Natural Resources, © Niagara Conservation Authority; 108 © Owen Bjorgan; 109 © Owen Bjorgan; 110 © Feng Yu/Shutterstock; 102 © Alan Watson; 112 © Owen Bjorgan; 113 © Owen Bjorgan; 114 © Owen Bjorgan; 115 © Owen Bjorgan; 116 © Nature Ontario; 117 © Owen Bjorgan; 119 top © pavels/Shutterstock; middle © suebmtl/Shutterstock; bottom © National Capital Commission; 120 © Critterbiz/Shutterstock; 121 © Bruce Di Labio; 122 © Frank B. Edwards; 123 © Frank B. Edwards; 124 © Kyle Horner; 125 © pavels/Shutterstock; 126 © Bonnechere Caves; 127 © Bonnechere Caves; 128 Chris Earley; 129 © National Capital Commission; 130 © Elbow Lake Education and Environment Centre; 131 © Elbow Lake Education and Environment Centre; 132 © Chris Earley; 133 © Frank B. Edwards; 134 © Hartley Millson; 135 top and bottom © Frank B. Edwards; 136 © suebmtl/Shutterstock; 137 © Nature Conservancy of Canada; 138 © Elliotte Rusty Harold/Shutterstock; 139 clockwise from top © Bruce Di Labio, © Martin P/Shutterstock, © Kletr/Shutterstock; 140 © Peggy deWitt; 141 © R.G. Rutkay; 142 © Janice McLean; 143 © Janice McLean; 144 © Joe Gilker/Dark Arts Astrophotography; 145 © Terence Dickinson; 146 © Janice McLean; 147 © Janice McLean; 149 © National Capital Commission; 150 © Kyle Horner; 151 © Hartley Millson; 152 © Chris Earley; 152 top © Frank B. Edwards; 152 bottom © Troy McMullin; 154 © Robert Spriggs/Shutterstock; 155 © marevos imaging/Shutterstock; 156 © Grant Dobson; 157 left © Gillian Shields; 157 right © Dana Shaw; 158 © Joe Bartok; 159 all photos © Joe Bartok; 160 © Bruce Di Labio; 161 clockwise from top left © Hartley Millson, © Elena Kreuzberg/CPAWS, © Bruce Di Labio; 162 © Owen Bjorgan; 163 left © Michael Cummings/Shutterstock; 163 right © Paul Beduhm/Gordon's Park Dark-Sky Preserve; 164 © Chris Earley; 165 © Chris Earley; 165 © Chris Earley; 166 © Chris Earley; 167 © Chiyacat/Shutterstock; 168 © Alan Watson; 170 © Ontario Nature; 171 top © Ray Ford/Ontario Nature; 171 bottom © Robert Hammer/Ontario Nature; 172 © Kyle Horner; 173 © Kyle Horner; 174 © Peter Kelly; 175 © Owen Bjorgan; 177 clockwise from top © Nature Conservancy of Canada, © Paul S. Wolf/Shutterstock, © Bill Macintyre/Nature Conservancy of Canada; 178 © Chris Earley; 179 © Ron Lohr; 180 © LianeM/Shutterstock; 181 © shipfactory/Shutterstock; 182 © Paul Beduhm/Gordon's Park Dark-Sky Preserve; 183 top and bottom © Paul Beduhm/Gordon's Park Dark-Sky Preserve; 184 © Marie Keates/www.iwalkalone.co.uk; 185 © Marie Keates/www.iwalkalone.co.uk; 186 © Michael Cummings/Shutterstock; 187 © marevos imaging/Shutterstock; 188 © Kyle Horner; 189 left © Kyle Horner; 189 right © Ontario Parks; 190 © Nature Conservancy of Canada; 191 © Nature Conservancy of Canada; 192 © Nottawasaga Valley Conservation Authority; 193 © Heather Kepran/Nottawasaga Valley Conservation Authority; 194 © Ontario Nature; 195 left and right © Chris Earley; 196 © Chris Earley; 197 © Ontario Parks; 199 © Saugeen Valley Conservation Authority; 200 © Kyle Horner; 201 © Ontario Parks; 202 © Joe Bartok; 203 © LesPalenik/Shutterstock; 204 © Jason Patrick Ross/Shutterstock; 205 © Alan Watson; 206 © Ryan Adams/Wye Marsh Wildlife Centre; 207 top and bottom © Wye Marsh Wildlife Centre; 208 clockwise from left © Ontario Parks; © Sharon Mollerus; © Ontario Parks; © Terry Alexander courtesy Ontario Nature; 210 © Terry Alexander courtesy Ontario Nature; 211 top and bottom © Ontario Parks; 212 © Ontario Parks; 213 top © Ontario Parks; 213 bottom © D. Gordon E. Robertson; 214 © Sharon Mollerus; 215 © Sharon Mollerus; 216 © Ontario Parks; 217 © Ontario Parks; 219 © Ontario Parks; 220 © Ontario Parks; 221 top © Ontario Parks; 221 bottom Paul Reeves Photography/Shutterstock.